The Memoirs of Alfred Hodgson

– EDITED BY KATHERINE HODGSON –

Printed and bound in England by www.printondemand-worldwide.com

http://www.fast-print.net/bookshop

THE MEMOIRS OF ALFRED HODGSON
Copyright © Alfred & Katherine Hodgson 2016

All rights reserved

No part of this book may be reproduced in any form by photocopying
or any electronic or mechanical means, including information storage
or retrieval systems, without permission in writing from both the
copyright owner and the publisher of the book.

The right of Alfred and Katherine Hodgson to be identified as the author and editor
respectively of this work has been asserted by them in accordance with the
Copyright, Designs and Patents Act 1988 and any subsequent amendments thereto.

A catalogue record for this book is available from the British Library

ISBN 978-178456-353-0

First published 2016 by
FASTPRINT PUBLISHING
Peterborough, England.

Contents

1.	Foreword	7
2.	Formative Years	11
3.	Maiden Voyage	22
4.	The Second Voyage: To the Spy Capital	37
5.	1942: On thin ice?	49
6.	The Third Voyage: Into the Breach	57
7.	The Fourth Voyage: From Cape Race to 'Cape Fear'	65
8.	The Fifth Voyage: On the Offensive	80
9.	The Sixth Voyage: The Sitting Duck	92
10.	The Naval Turning Point: Farewell to the 'Happy Time'	105
11.	The Seventh Voyage: D Day and Beyond	121
12.	The Eighth Voyage: The Beginning of the End	132
13.	The Ninth Voyage: The End	143
14.	The Tenth Voyage: Clearing up	160
15.	Conclusion	163

Edited by Katherine Hodgson

'The Battle of the Atlantic was the dominating factor all through the war. Never for one moment could we forget that everything happening elsewhere, on land, at sea, or in the air, depended ultimately on its outcome, and amid all other cares we viewed its changing fortunes day by day with hope or apprehensions.'[1]

Winston Churchill

---

[1] B.B. Schofield, 'The Defeats of the U-Boats during World War II,' Journal of Contemporary History, Vol 16, The Second World War: Part 1, (1981) p.119

Edited by Katherine Hodgson

Foreword

'I was always attracted to the idea of being at sea. I liked the thought of it. The RAF was new and unknown, the Navy always appealed to me.'

This was the simple response my grandfather gave me when asked why he enrolled in the Merchant Navy in 1941. He was dispatched on his first voyage in September of that year, aged only eighteen, and spent a further five years at sea. His answer paints a picture of a young adolescent; eager and naïve. A picture of a teenager who had an idealistic, almost romantic, depiction of naval life. It was a powerful relationship he had with the navy. It was based on a genuine fondness for the ocean, for the travel and for the force. Now today – aged 93 – the same fondness remains, albeit in a less powerful sense.

It can be hard to understand why this would be the case. Alfred Hodgson was a Radio Officer on ten voyages, each with a different ship, a different crew and a different destination. One might presume he endured loneliness and had a distressingly unstable time. Yet he did not. To my grandfather, life at sea was artificial: not a life of great anxiety and instability. It was one of variety, rather than loneliness: a variety of sights; sounds; smells and people. He talks fondly of the camaraderie on board – the familial spirit and the need to 'all group together.' They were 'all in it together'.

And yet it was not all happy. I cannot, and he cannot, portray his war memoirs through rose tinted spectacles. Death was constantly lurking. It was something he was aware of all the time – and so were his fellow crewmen. They just had to get on with it. That idea of 'just getting on with it' strikes at the very heart of this story. The time he and his fellow seamen spent at sea was one of perseverance, determination and sheer courage.

'Living history' – my grandfather's quotes, memories and opinions – embody much of this book. A primary, *living* source is a raw form of history. It can tackle a specific event or period with a degree of poignancy and emotion that many secondary sources cannot. But it can also convey a sense of emotion which other primary sources – stripped of a living narrator – cannot. Therefore, most of this story is written in first person, the words straight from my grandfather. His experience sits alongside historical debate and research. An academic and systematic addition to what is, essentially, a very personal story and way of writing.

'History is written by the victors' – a phrase commonly attributed to Churchill. Churchill's mammoth six volume collection *A History of the Second World War*, was an extremely profitable and highly influential take on WWII. It painted the British war leader in the most esteemed light, moulding facts to do so. To this day, Churchill is widely accepted as an infallible and genuinely untouchable political and military leader. His efforts and work should not be diminished in importance. But any errors he ever made, or flaws that he had, are often glossed over. The ex-Prime Minister has his books to thank for much of that. If this brief digression proves anything, then it's this: history is entirely dependent on the historian's interpretation of it. I do not have a bias in favour of the Navy. Some may debate, to no real value or outcome, about which Force was most important during the war. It is a frivolous debate to engage in. WW2 was a total war – fought on all three theatres of battle: land; sea and air. All three armed forces were equally as important as the other. It is highly unfair to glorify one above the other when so many sacrificed their lives for the Allied Forces.

However, total war is so much more than the military. It's the collective efforts of the population, working together to defeat a common enemy. It's the workers in the factories making the munitions; it's the mothers suddenly in the workplace filling the previously male dominated jobs. It's the household vegetable plots, the blackouts, the home guard and the anti-air raid wardens. It's those in the country opening up their homes to vulnerable children. Reading this list, one would not be blamed for assuming that war left Britain a resilient and united people. Resilient? - yes. But social unity was not achieved. The ever-present class system remained a relentless burden on social justice, and sexism and poverty had yet to be properly addressed.

The following focuses on one man's time at sea. It simply tells a story, highlighting true historical facts and interpreting the war in an honest manner.

It is worth noting this: the Merchant Navy played a vital role throughout the war's six years. It supplied an island nation, unable to self-provide, with much needed resources. As Merchant vessel after Merchant vessel was torpedoed in the North Atlantic, Britain was slowly suffocating. The Battle of the Atlantic – the longest running battle of the Second World War – was hugely important. The death rate of Merchant seamen is estimated at 17% (approximately 33,000 men) higher than the other armed forces.[2] The Battle of the Atlantic was a closely fought one. For the men of the Merchant Navy it was one of the most dangerous battles they could be part of.

Katherine Hodgson

---

[2] Ibid, p.128

2 – Formative Years

It was a great tradition in 1920s Edinburgh for families to walk the length of the Esplanade to the Floral Clock, at the Mound in West Princes Street Gardens. I would walk this with my father, mother and sister every Sunday. My older brother, Reg, spent much of his childhood at boarding school. On Sundays, I felt a great sense of pride when we walked as a family. I had plenty of confidence and boyhood zeal as I strolled along in my sharpest navy suit and black leather 'Kid gloves'. My mother, ever the epitome of high fashion, was consistently bedecked in the most splendid of hats. They were complete with feather boas, layers of lace, netting and felt rims. Her headgear was frequently complimented. I still remember glancing up at my father, leading his flock through the city. His imposing stature, trademark bowler hat and rolled umbrella used to fill me with admiration. My father had been a Cumberland wrestler in his youth. His grandiose height and build undoubtedly dwarfed my mother who, for her time, was exceptionally tall at 5ft10. Weekends were special and we often spent Saturdays exploring the city and its surrounding areas. We would visit a variety of attractions: Portobello Beach, the zoo, Dreghorn Barracks or further afield to North Berwick. A firm favourite of mine was a visit to Dalmeny Estate across the river. We would take the ferry at Cramond and then wander through the Estate to South Queensferry and the Forth Bridge. Evenings were spent in the comfort of our home, listening to my mother playing the grand piano or looking at images through the Magic Lantern. This was an early image projector which reflected light from an oil or gas lamp on to a condensing lens. The lens focused the light on to the slide which then projected the image, much like a modern projector.

I had a comfortable and enjoyable childhood. Despite this, I was not totally sheltered. I was not oblivious to the social tensions of the time. From a young age I was aware of inner city violence and crime, of social inequality, and of sectarian division. My mother was quick to tell me which parts of Edinburgh I could freely wander through. She designated 'no go' areas for me, and this limited the routes I could take when travelling alone. No back streets or alleys, main roads only. One walk I liked to take by myself was from our home to the Public Library. I was by no-means an avid reader but I was a regular visitor to the library on George V Bridge. The exterior was imposing and the interior was sacrosanct. Talking was only allowed at a whisper and only when absolutely essential. On every book the publishers' binding had been removed and replaced by a leather cover embossed in the name of 'Edinburgh Public Library'. People treated the library like they would a church – it was a holy shrine to the great writers of the past and the most treasured books of humanity. In the 1930s the library was one of the few places where women were in charge. Librarians were predominantly female and yielded the power to silence you, charge you for late returns or remove you from the premises. What fascinated me most about the Library was how it differed from the rest of society. It had an unusually exuberant style and design, a rigid and almost totalitarian attitude, and was a space with a dominant female presence. The Library opposed the norms of the outside world.

I was largely able to enjoy my childhood because of my parents' financial security. Being a member of the middle classes meant the Depression had less of an adverse impact on our household income. The working classes tended to get hit the hardest. In 1928, shortly before the Crash, salaries for clerical staff, businessmen, professionals and other white collar workers did decrease marginally. But these salaries had all fully returned to their pre-Depression levels by 1936. Overall, there was only a slight variation in middle class incomes during the Depression, with taxation rates remaining relatively stable.[3] The cost of living for the average middle class individual in January 1939, was in fact less than what it had been in January 1923. Despite this relative privilege, I was aware of the grossly debilitating economic situation for millions of Britons. The 1930s witnessed a series of unemployment riots. I still vividly remember the headlines regarding the Jarrow March. In October 1936, 200 unemployed men marched from Jarrow to London. The protesters marched to show Parliament that more had to be done to combat unemployment in

---

[3] R. McKibbin, 'Classes and Cultures, England 1918-1951,' (New York, 1998) p.59

the North. In some areas unemployment was as high as 70%[4]. The Jarrow marchers campaigned to have their local shipyard reopened. The demise of old, heavy industry and the economic crisis had led the marchers into poverty. Along with their MP Ellen Wilkinson, it led them to use radical and bold tactics in the fight for social justice.

By summer 1939 I was sixteen years old. I had just left school, finishing on a high with a superlative report. This boosted my ego and cocooned me into that nauseating teenage complacency. The type which allowed me to spend weeks floating around the city socialising with friends. That was then followed by weeks relaxing in bed, munching on home-baked biscuits and reading for a few hours at a time. Although that summer brought me much joy and tranquillity, it was an internationally tense period for Britain. The beginning of the year marked an increasing number of anti-British speeches by Hitler. This led Chamberlain to finally initiate light, temporary conscription – a year after the Secretary of State for War, Leslie Hore-Belisha, had originally requested it. South-east England was subjected to practice black-outs in early 1939. In January, Stalin and Hitler began discussions over a possible Nazi-Soviet alliance. Discussions of the same nature involving the Allies and Stalin did not begin until as

---

[4] C. Collette, 'The Jarrow Crusade', (2011), BBC History
http://www.bbc.co.uk/history/british/britain_wwone/jarrow_01.s html

late as April.[5] Britain had 'missed the bus'[6] in terms of gaining a Soviet ally, and allowed two of the most feared dictators to grow worryingly closer. Mussolini caused the liberal nations further anxiety in spring 1939. The Italian leader occupied Albania in April of that year. The threat of fascism thus peaked the following month when the Pact of Steel was signed.[7] By July 1939, most British people knew that war was approaching. The Civil Defence Act was passed and a further 39 million gas masks were deployed along with one million Anderson shelters. With masks being produced at a rate of 150,000 per week from 1937, a total of 38 million gas masks were available to the public in 1938 alone. Despite all these warning signs, it would be a particularly ominous family gathering at

---

[5] It's worth noting that the British government deliberately took their talks with the Russians slowly due to Chamberlain's 'profound distrust' of Russia. He refused to talk to Stalin personally or send the Foreign Secretary, Lord Halifax. Instead a minor civil servant was sent to Moscow by slow boat with orders to 'go slowly' with discussions. In comparison, the German Foreign Minister Ribbentrop visited Stalin and his aides and hurried to Moscow on 23rd August 1939 to sign the Nazi-Soviet Pact.

[6] On April 4th 1940 Neville Chamberlain told the House of Commons that Hitler had 'missed the bus' in terms of creating a combative and, ultimately, successful war for Germany. Chamberlain had spoken too soon. Only five days later Norway was invaded by the Nazis, and the so-called Phoney War gradually came to a close.

[7] The Pact stated that both countries would support one and other if either entered into a war.

our Joppa home to finally make me appreciate how fast approaching war truly was.[8]

* * *

The sun streamed through the trees as we took our seats at the garden table. My mother had prepared a fine looking spread: cured meats; smoked fish; freshly baked warm bread; potato salad; crispy white lettuce and rocket. At the end of the table sat dessert: a brightly coloured fruit salad of berries; ice cold vanilla ice cream and crunchy biscuits having only just been whipped out of the oven a few minutes earlier.

'The Battleships in the River Forth are moving out of Rosyth.' My father commented as he helped himself to some potato salad.

'That's a sure sign that they're preparing for war.' My uncle Bill agreed. Bill had been a civil servant in South Africa for many years. He lived with the O'Callaghan family – the late Mr O'Callaghan was one of his closest friends. Mrs O'Callaghan had joined my Uncle Bill when he stayed in Britain in 1938 and 1939. By this point, Bill was retired and looking forward to spending his retirement in London. When war broke out he made his arrangements to return to South Africa and reside with the O'Callaghan family once more. In 1940 Mrs O'Callaghan wrote to me, inviting me to seek refuge from the war and live with them:

---

[8] A suburb of Edinburgh

Darling Alfy,

My heart is very sore today, but God will help me to see you again, for you are coming next year with your Uncle Willie to me. You are, you must.

Till then, Alfy.

J.B.O'Callaghan

As the lunch continued the conversation grew increasingly dark. Although it pained my relatives to say so, 1939 was a turning point for everyone and appeasement was no longer the easy option. People couldn't, and wouldn't, laugh off German aggression like they had in previous years. In March 1936 Hitler occupied the Rhineland but the only lasting memory I have of that is a contemporary music hall joke. In it, Hitler was quoted as saying 'I will supply the world with bacon if you will only let me keep the Rhine.' When the Spanish Civil War broke out in July 1936 and Hitler, Mussolini and Stalin involved themselves, I saw it as nothing more than a battle between Communism and capitalism. Hardly a threat to Britain. The following year, when the Luftwaffe decimated Guernica and Madrid, I failed to realise just how dangerous such a powerful and destructive Nazi Air Force could be. In 1938 Austria was annexed and again it was only too easy to brush this off with racial ignorance, claiming that Austria was peopled by Germans anyway.

The summer of 1939 was the first time my entire family would assemble together, with relatives from Scotland, Ireland and England. It was the last time such a gathering would occur. On 1st September Germany invaded Poland. On 3rd September Britain declared war on Germany, with France making the same declaration the following day.

* * *

In June 1940 I joined the Local Defence Volunteers (LDV). The French occupation caused widespread fear of a German invasion of Britain. Although the chances of Germany successfully invading Britain were extremely low (if not impossible), the need for decent civil defence intensified. On 14th May the newly appointed Secretary of State for War, Anthony Eden, broadcast a message calling for men to join their LDV:

'We want large numbers of such men in Great Britain who are British subjects, between the ages of seventeen and sixty-five, to come forward now and offer their services in order to make assurance [that an invasion would be repelled] doubly sure. The name of the new force which is now to be raised will be the Local Defence Volunteers. This name describes its duties in three words. You will not be paid, but you will receive uniforms and will be armed. In order to volunteer, what you have to do is give your name at your local police station, and then, when we want you, we will let you know.'[9]

After joining the LDV, it was several weeks before proper uniforms arrived. When they did I wore a basic uniform: a standard khaki Army coat; cap; boots and

---
[9] http://www.home-guard.org.uk/hg/hgfaq.html

trousers. At first, equipment was rather primitive as the War Office desperately scrounged abroad for weaponry. We often had to make do with outdated WWI guns. In July 1940, Churchill changed the name of the LDV to the better known 'Home Guard.' Slowly, but surely, the force became more organised and better equipped. I enjoyed learning how to use a rifle and make a Molotov Cocktail. We had endless drills and parades, with some scathing criticism from the Regular Army instructors. I also trained as a firewatcher and took my turn on a duty rota. Despite the lack of resources, the outdated equipment and the Home Guard's bad reputation, I felt a great sense of pride when I was on duty. I was simply pleased to be part of the war effort. Somewhat overlooked, the Home Guard played an important role in the British war effort. A total of 1206 men lost their lives volunteering for the Home Guard.[10] They worked hard to maintain order and safety during the Guard's four year tenure. Those volunteers were prepared to sacrifice their lives just as troops abroad did.

Growing up, I had no real vision of a career. My mother thought accountancy would be a good option, and I couldn't think of anything better. I needed more qualifications if I was to go to University and study accountancy. Thus, I enrolled in a college where I could obtain the required University Prelims. By September 1940 I had the necessary certificates. My mother introduced me to a senior partner at Howden and Molleson, a firm based in Edinburgh and one of

---

[10] Figures obtained from BBC History website and articles

the original firms of Scottish Chartered Accountants. I began working for them at £12 per year while my father paid out 100 guineas as the entry premium. I was contracted to complete a five year apprenticeship. My employment was not exactly exciting and I quickly grew restless. I wanted to join the Navy as a Royal Navy Reserve wireless cadet. Shortly after turning eighteen, I sent my application. While awaiting a response from the Navy I enrolled at a Wireless College.

* * *

During the Phoney War my mother and I watched, from our front door, what we thought was an air force training operation. It wasn't until later that we learned that it was a real dogfight with German aircraft. One German plane was shot down. The next day I picked up a flattened bullet from the doorstep, lying in the exact spot where we had been. A few days later I went to St Philips Church, opposite our house, to attend the Lying in State of the German pilot. I still have that flattened bullet. I keep it as a souvenir. It also acts as a reminder that I could have easily joined that pilot, but without the ceremony.

* * *

By August 1941 there was still no word from the Navy regarding my application. That same month I passed my exam at the Wireless College and signed the Official Secrets Act. I was 18 and impervious to the wise note of caution from my family. I decided that if the Royal Navy did not want me then the

Merchant Navy did. The ink was hardly dry on my application before I was given my first posting on 17th September 1941. My first voyage would mark my departure from cosy adolescence and into the brutal world of warfare and adulthood.

3 – *Maiden Voyage*

<u>The SS Kingswood</u>: 5080 tonnage (gross) vessel, operating from 1939 to 1943. It met its fate on 17.12.1943, torpedoed off the West coast of Africa by the U515. The entire crew of 48 are believed to have survived.

The Memoirs of Alfred Hodgson

A hand delivered telegram arrived with brief instructions:

> 'Report to the Shipping Office at Methil in Fife on 20/09/1941.'

Those words created a surge of excitement within me – excitement at the unknown, at the exhilarating action that lay ahead. Those words *now* read as an empty and detached confirmation that very soon I would be part of a violent and dangerous struggle for survival. Those words, void of any emotion, lined the scrap of paper in a haunting fashion. No best wishes, no words of advice. Just orders, plain and simple orders. I would very quickly learn that total war meant learning to accept these solemn, and often harsh, orders.

When I arrived at Methil I was told the first ship I would be sailing on was the SS Kingswood. The names of ships were screened to the public during wartime so this information had to remain strictly confidential. My first voyage was to the Gold Coast, Western Africa. This conjured up a romantic and fantastical image of a Rider Haggard novel. Having always been one of my favourite authors, I was thrilled at the prospect of actually being able to re-enact the part of his characters. I fantasized about discovering some undiscovered region of Africa, just like my fictional hero Allan Quartermain. Seeing and touching the wild animals, drinking from the springs, camping in the desert. It all effortlessly played out in my mind like watching a glitzy Hollywood film.

All of my mail was censored on joining the Merchant Navy. Signing on at the Shipping Office, a bundle of letters was quickly handed to me. One of them was the long awaited response from the Royal Navy calling me for an interview. It would have been my first choice, but now as a fully-fledged Radio Officer in training it wasn't easy to just switch. The Captain, Fredrick H Parmee, told me that it would be possible to have my assignment cancelled so I could attend the interview. That was hardly the straight forward or preferred option. By then my mind was also full of images of the Gold Coast: of hazy, pink sunsets and long stretches of soft yellow sand. As much as the Royal Navy seemed like the perfect choice for a war hungry teenager fond of the sea, I couldn't leave my post now. Africa awaited me and I felt a tinge of resentment at the Royal Navy for its dilatory response. I decided to wait until I returned and go for an interview during my next leave.

Stepping onto the Kingswood I was not entirely sure what to expect. How did the ship operate exactly? What was the daily schedule like? How would the other men act? Yet I quickly found myself very impressed with the welcoming atmosphere and cleanliness. I even had a cabin to myself. On board there was a Senior Radio Officer and me, his junior. A ship would ideally have three radio officers. This meant the twenty four hour watch could be equally split. Each officer spent four lonely hours out on 'watch' for any signs of U Boat activity. He then had a break from the painstakingly dull task of peering into a telescope, and instead spent four hours on radio watch. Initially, I was absorbed in merely learning the ropes: visual signalling on the Aldis Lamp and signal flags; the basic radio watch; and regular decoding of constant instructions from the Admiralty. There was much to learn. The Aldis Lamp was like a big flash lamp which used Morse code to spell out letters. Each letter of the alphabet had its own symbol. The lamp had a magnifying glass behind the bulb. This projected the symbols directly into the view of the person whom the message was intended for. It was easy enough to use but practice was needed and it was a slow, laborious process as you spelt out words letter by letter. Despite my formal training at the Wireless College I was not prepared for the speed and efficiency required at sea. On neighbouring ships, Royal Navy visual signallers had the precision and skill which newcomers like myself could only dream of. Thankfully, they were patient with us.

Maintaining the equipment was fairly straightforward. It mostly consisted of cleaning and topping up the radios' batteries. Since the Kingswood was a coal burner I also had the task of cleaning off the grime from the aerial insulators. These were wires connected to the radios and were exposed to all weather, stretching above the deck. Perhaps of greatest importance was the job I was expected to undertake in the event of the ship sinking. I was tasked with putting the secret decoding books into a weighted bag and throwing them overboard. They would thus be destroyed and unable to reach enemy intelligence. I would then put the portable radio transmitter into a suitable lifeboat and check back to the radio cabin to see whether the Senior Radio Officer needed any help in sending out a distress message. Then I would wait for further orders. Further orders which could have been to find my allocated lifeboat and flee for safety, or remain working as the mammoth vessel submerged. I found comfort in the thought that if – and most probably when – such an occurrence where to happen, I would be able to flee fairly promptly. This was merely because I naively assumed I would have little to do once I had reported back to the radio cabin.

The ship traded from Middlesbrough in peacetime and the regular crew all came from that area. There was a strong familial spirit between the regular crew. I knew I was not the same as them; my career was not on the water. I was a Supernumerary. 'Round the clock radio watch at sea' was something new for wartime – hence the additional radio officers. The men, however, were generally a friendly bunch. We all tended to group with whoever we were working with at any given time.

The following day the Kingswood sailed to Oban. It left Oban on 23rd September en route to Freetown, Sierra Leone. We were to meet the rest of our convoy in Liverpool. We sailed along the east coast of Scotland, through the Pentland Firth to the assembly point. On arrival at Liverpool we encountered thirty or so ships, all part of the convoy. I realised that my uncle Bill, who was returning to South Africa, would be travelling on one of the accompanying passenger liners. I looked up the convoy schedules and found his ship. As the legion of ships set sail I remember wistfully looking over at his liner – positioned in the outer flanks of the convoy – and feeling disappointed at not being able to make contact with him.

Sailing from Liverpool to Freetown meant sailing south west. We sailed along the outer edges of the Bay of Biscay (home to eight U Boat flotillas by 1942). This region was crawling with submarines and like most coastal zones, loaded with dangerous underwater mines. Escaping the dangers of the Bay of Biscay, we then skimmed the coast of Portugal and made haste for mid-west Africa. The journey was a relatively uneventful one, with only a handful of 'alarms' (notifications from the Commodore that a change in route was needed) and 'diversions' (altering the route appropriately). At that time, the Kriegsmarine was not heavily invested in this particular area. U Boats stayed away, concentrated in the North Atlantic. Surface raiders were the predominant German presence along the western coasts in autumn 1941. The notorious 'Hipper' was lurking in the waters before Freetown.[11] The KMS Admiral Hipper was a maritime beast. It sank the HMS Glowworm in April 1940 and, along with two other cruisers and four destroyers, eliminated three allied vessels as part of Operation Juno a mere two months later. The Hipper was a feared beast. We thanked God that we never encountered it on our route. Most of our problems arose in the Takoradi Approach area, where the French had planted numerous mines.

* * *

---

[11] Admiral Hipper- heavy cruiser. Displacement 18,200T, speed: 32 kts. Armament: 8×8" and 12×4.1" guns

The saloon was filled with smoke and the deafening sound of chatter. I grabbed a cup of milky tea and a hot roll and sat down at a table by the porthole. Slowly sipping my tea and nibbling on my roll, I gazed out at the sea; to the waves twisting and turning erratically. The doors to the saloon were thrown open and six, stout middle aged men strolled in. Loud shrieks of laughter accompanied them. Engrossed in their evidently hilarious conversation they proceeded to sit down beside me. Despite being a cargo ship the Kingswood had six private cabins and these were occupied by British planters going back to their estates in Africa.

'Good morning,' they all chimed.

'Where do you get the tea?' one asked, frantically scanning the saloon for evidence of hot beverages.

'Up at the back, on the table at the far left.' I replied, nodding in the direction of the table. On it sat two large heated containers of black tea, several jugs of milk and a couple of ramekin dishes filled with sugar cubes.

The man, dressed in loose cotton trousers, open toed sandals and a floaty white shirt smiled at me appreciatively. 'Shall I bring back a cup for everyone here?' he asked loudly.

His friends all murmured in agreement and began to light up their cigarettes and pipes as he walked off.

'I'm sure you'll be glad to get home.' I said to the group as I finished my roll.

'Of course,' one replied through a screen of smoke. 'We live in a beautiful place, you'll soon see that.'

'I'm looking forward to it.' 'Is this your first voyage then?' another one asked curiously. I nodded and gulped down the last of my tea. Staring into the cup only the dregs remained. 'Drink up, have more.' A loud voice boomed above me as a second cup was thrust before me.

'I did say I would get tea for everyone here,' the man said as I looked up at him in surprise.

'Thank you.'

'I'm Walter,' he said, handing out the last cup to his friend at the far end of the table. Walter proceeded to sit down across from me.

'Alfred.'

The other five men began to introduce themselves.

'We were just discussing the recent royal visit from Edward VIII before we came in,' explained Walter, who appeared as leader of this apparent clique.

'Quite the scandal,' concurred another.

Walter grinned at me and said, 'This is worth listening to.'

And so the six planters each began to tell me a different part of the story. Each lavished over every salacious detail in the often embarrassing, and terribly obscene, plotline. They howled as the gossiping came to a natural end.

'You couldn't make it up.' Walter said finishing the tale.

* * *

By the time we reached Africa I found the heat rather uncomfortable. The blackout regulations required that the portholes were closed at all times after dark. As there was no air conditioning, at evening the ship became very stuffy. I compensated by taking my mattress on to the deck and slept there but it was only later that I realised how unorthodox this was. I was lucky to have such a tolerant Captain for my first voyage.

As we rounded the bulge of North West Africa, orders came in to break off from the convoy and head for the Gulf of Guinea. For the first time in three weeks we saw land, and not just a vague shoreline in the distance. It was a comforting sight – to actually set foot on ground would be an entirely different, albeit better, experience. We were to stop in Ghana at the Takoradi port in the municipal city of Sekondi-Takoradi. Edging into the bay at Takoradi we found another naval vessel already stopped there. There was no harbour so we dropped anchor. On doing so, we immediately attracted dozens of local 'bum boats' of every size and shape. All the little fishing boats were fully loaded with fruit and natives hungry for a sale. They came aboard without haste and I soon learned why we had been told to seal our portholes despite the stifling heat. An open porthole meant a long arm would suddenly appear and scoop up anything and everything in sight. I bought numerous wicker baskets and far more fruit than I could eat. It did not cost me any money as I paid with old copies of the Saturday Evening Post.[12] On a later visit to Takoradi the locals refused our cheap offer of magazines, instead demanding half a crown in hard cash from everybody. They had previously received a visit from an American ship. One exception to the new hard cash rule was 'English cigarettes' with the locals preferring British cigarettes to the American brands. Although I smoked very little I kept a good supply of British cigarettes for currency.

Stopping at Takoradi for the first time I was desperate to go ashore and explore the land. Strictly speaking the crew was not supposed to leave the ship. However, being a precocious youngster I managed to persuade Captain Parmee to grant me a shore pass. My Sunday obligation was cited as the reason for my amphibious adventure. It was a genuine excuse. I sought comfort in religion and had a great need to attend Mass, even though I was intent on touring as well. I was lucky that Parmee was a tolerant Captain who had not yet got used to the new, inexperienced type of crew. The naval ship at Takoradi had a pilot boat and this, in addition to the boat from our own shipping agent, provided the facilities to get to the shore and back. At first I was very impressed that the naval pilot boat would come and collect me right

---

[12] A colourful US magazine especially for service personnel supplied by a few charitable organizations

away. I later learned that the seaman operating the boat was so bored that he welcomed any excuse to run across to the pier. Dismounting the pilot boat and stepping onto land, I clutched my Mission to Seaman Booklet. In it was a list of almost every port in the world, with the locations of missionaries nearby who would assist any seaman in need. Surveying the area, the only sign of habitation seemed to be the local missionary which my booklet directed me to. I proceeded to enter it and meet the cleric in charge. A man dressed in the most vibrant, bright and mesmerizing layers of red, gold and blue cotton sat above me in what appeared to be a throne. I started to introduce myself and speak briefly about religion. I was, after all, intending to go to Mass. When I began to discuss the Mass itself our conversation was brought to a sudden but courteous close. I never found out what the dazzling cleric's religion was, but it was certainly not Catholicism. The cleric summoned a driver, arranged for him to take me to the Christian mission station and told me the currency in cigarettes to give him.

Thus followed one of the most memorable car rides of my life. The barefoot driver of a rather ramshackle vehicle drove through the jungle, on a dirt track that could never be called a road. Whizzing cross country in the vehicle, dust sprung into my eyes and stung my skin. Despite this discomfort all my naive, childhood dreams of a jungle life became real. We passed shrieking monkeys swinging from branches and lions napping under the burning orange sun. We saw multi-coloured flowers glitter under the sunlight and big, beautiful birds glide through the clear blue sky. Suddenly, the car burst into a clearing and there sat four men in white robes drinking beer from pint glasses. These were the Catholic 'White Fathers' (now known as the Missionaries of Africa). I have no recollection of the Church or the services that I attended but I do remember being sent to the house of an affluent local planter. There, I had an insight into the luxuries afforded to the privileged white colonialists. This planter lived in a high quality, large bungalow filled with servants and excessive quantities of food and drink.

From the White Fathers' station the port of Sekondi was only a short distance away. The missionaries arranged for me to go on a tour of the local area. It did not take long to absorb the Mission Station, the nearby school and witness the locals hard at work. Their main occupations included offshore fishing from sampans and working on the sugar plantations. The schools concentrated on the traditional 'three R's' – reading, writing and arithmetic. Their equipment was minimal. Leading me through the classrooms, overflowing with glassy eyed young children, a teacher explained to me a typical day in the missionary run school. The walk back to the ship was a colourful and entertaining one. Locals filled the Sekondi streets with vibrant and loud parades, performing on their Ashanti drums and effortlessly dancing along to the fast paced beat. When I first visited Africa, I was a young, excitable man. Like many others of my age and nationality, I fetishized Africa. I overlooked its place as a large, important continent, filled with numerous different cultures, ethnicities and demographics. Perhaps this has shaped how I recall this visit. Perhaps my interpretation of the continent, at that time, has caused me to remember it in a *predominantly* rural, and primitive way.

After a few days we left Sekondi-Takoradi port and headed for Freetown. Gazing at the map, I presumed that Freetown was just around the corner but in reality it was quite a distance (a total of almost 2000 km). Freetown had been converted to a naval base and convoy centre. The Armed Forces were very much in evidence and the harbour was protected by a Boom to keep out submarines.[13] The anchorage was dominated by the Union Castle liner, the Edinburgh Castle,[14] which was being used as a naval and airforce headquarter and base for accommodation. Docked alongside the shore the saying goes that the Edinburgh Castle was immovable because it was resting on a bed of empty bottles.

---

[13] Typically a net strung across water to prevent enemy ships navigating that particular stretch of water.

[14] The Union Castle Line of ships were prominent passenger and cargo ships travelling between Britain and South Africa from 1900-1977. The Edinburgh Castle was the second ship of the class to have that name. It was built in 1910 and was an armed merchant cruiser in the Great War. During WW2, the Admiralty purchased the cruiser and used it as an accommodation barge in Freetown. At the end of the war the Edinburgh Castle was sunk 60 miles off the coast of Freetown by gunfire and depth charges from the HMS Fal and HMS Porchester Castle. A third Edinburgh Castle was completed in 1948.

We were then instructed to sail up river for approximately twenty miles to pick up a cargo of copra.[15] This journey involved the hideous copra beetle[16] which emerged in swarms of thousands. The copra beetle is a tiny dark insect and therefore hard to spot. It made life rather uncomfortable because we would all easily swallow these minuscule bugs and find them covering everything – not just our food. The copra was carried on board in sacks. This was undertaken by hundreds of local workers who hurried along the beaches into barges, where they emptied the barges by the sack-full. The work was labour intensive but labour was very cheap and plentiful. The crew were lucky: we did not have to help move the copra sacks. This difficult, undesirable task was passed onto the natives. The heat was stifling, the insects were everywhere and the land was dry and fairly barren. The ship was uncomfortably warm. There was a fan in the saloon which gave some respite but not much. To pass the time I used to sit in the saloon, enjoying the dulcet tones of Vera Lynn over the radio. But at least I was inside and unworked: unlike the locals outside, I was not undertaking physically exerting work under the baking sun. I got off easy in this instance.

Within a few days the ship returned to the Freetown anchorage and joined a convoy for the

---

[15] Copra is the dried kernel of a coconut and is used to extract coconut oil. It's usually ground and then boiled to allow the oil to be taken.
[16] The necrobia rufipes, otherwise known as the red-legged ham beetle or copra beetle, is an insect which attacks high protein products such as copra, ham and also bone.

journey home. The trip back to Britain was a relatively pain-free one. The convoy escorts guided us safely and efficiently. We only endured the occasional zig-zag diversion. We returned to Tyneside on December 17th 1941. I was signed off for home leave and returned to Scotland in time for the festivities. As I graced the steps to my Edinburgh family home, I held in my hands African wicker baskets filled with left-over fruit. In my bag resided many Christmas treats, particularly heavily rationed goods – sugar, sweets, biscuits and bananas – all of which were well received by my family.

4 – The Second Voyage: To the Spy Capital

The SS Holmbury: a 4556 (gross) tonnage steam boat, completed in 1925 in Port Glasgow. The ship was owned by Alexander Capper & Co Ltd, London. The SS Holmbury was sunk in the Atlantic on 15th May 1943. It met its fate en route from Montevideo to Freetown, after being hit by a torpedo and 26 rounds of gunfire from the U-Boat U-123. The Holmbury was without a convoy.

December 17th – December 31st 1941 was the short extent of my leave. A Christmas break which ended all too soon. New Year's Eve marked the beginning of my second voyage and on that cold winter's morning I travelled to Newcastle to join the SS Holmbury.

On arrival at Newcastle I received the news that the destination was to be Lisbon, Portugal – the notorious 'Spy Capital' of the World. This nickname had been penned a couple of years before war had broken out, the result of Portugal's neutral stance in the face of growing international tensions. The Portuguese people had already picked their sides, some favoured the Allies, some the Axis forces. Others didn't care either way – money was to be made in selling information from servicemen. This meant that we were all to be vetted by the Intelligence Section of the Foreign Office, to weed out any risky personnel who should not be allowed into potential enemy territory. I was still a teenager and the idea of entering the cloak and dagger world of international espionage was stuff of slick Hollywood films. The individual briefing by the Foreign Office was quite impressive. The FO staff came on board and interrogated us individually. They took away all my papers: my identity card; Ministry of Shipping documents; all my textbooks on electricity and radio communications; and any other piece of paper which might conceivably provide information to the enemy. This was the only voyage where such precautions were taken. I should say now, I never came across any allied seamen prepared to sell information to spies. Ever.

As a group we were instructed on how to behave in what we should consider to be hostile territory. 'You should always go ashore in a group and never stray away as individuals...You will be plagued, bribed, coerced, threatened to give away information – but always remain resolute...'

At the time I never understood what information I had which could actually be of interest to the Third Reich. Regardless, any information could be in some way valuable and the standard government guideline was 'don't talk.' I had no idea why we were going to Lisbon and we were never told, this was significantly indicative of the power the British Government had. We never questioned the motives or intentions: we just acted.

Upon departure we were told we would be stopping in Spanish Morocco, at a port called Melilla. There, we would collect a cargo of iron ore. Iron ore was a primary ingredient in the production of munitions and in constant demand in Britain. After this was announced I frantically scanned my old school atlas in search of the exotic sounding destination. Melilla is just opposite the southern coast of Spain. Not only did this indicate that my geography needed brushing up, but that we would be stopping in Gibraltar. Gibraltar, another destination I had long wished to see. Yet again this ignited visions straight from a story book adventure. My duties on the Holmbury were the same as before. This time, however, there were three radio officers – spreading the work out neatly and giving me some welcomed extra sleep. The route went as so: we hugged the coast around the Pentland Firth; then onto the Western Isles where we took refuge in Tobermory at Bloody Bay, in the Isle of Mull. There was a boom across this bay and it was used as an assembly point for convoys and a training area for escorts. We had to get inside the boom before dark. The Kriegsmarine had discovered that the U-Boats could avoid detection by ASDIC if they only partially submerged and sailed on the surface. Obviously if the U-Boats followed this strategy in daylight they would be seen, hence the need to take shelter before nightfall.

From Mull we headed south to Liverpool. There, we sought shelter behind a boom in the main convoy assembly point. Entry and exit from the booms was quite complex, a result of the humiliating attack at Scapa Flow in 1939.[17] Booms were like air locks – the entrance was divided into sections and depending on which boom you went to, and where it was based, there could be several sections. The division was created by the gate wire netting which sunk to the seabed, stopping ships and underwater vessels gaining access. If the Navy needed to let an allied vessel into the boom they would raise the netting. The newly entered ships would then be in one section of the boom, and checks were made to ensure no U Boats

---

[17] Scapa Flow is a natural harbour in the Orkney Islands, Scotland. During the war it was used a main base for many naval vessels. From here, many convoys departed for Murmansk. On October 13th 1939 the U-Boat -47, commanded by Lt. Gunther Prien, slipped past Orkney and into the harbour. There it waited underwater until the HMS Royal Oak was spotted in the early hours of October 14th. The U-Boat fired torpedoes and the Royal Oak capsized, killing 833 men.

slipped in. Afterwards the second section would be opened and the procedure would continue. We left Liverpool as part of a convoy headed for Gibraltar. The convoy sailed right into the epicentre of the war at sea. German planes and U-Boats were everywhere: constantly harassing us and forcing the ship to take multiple diversions. These course diversions were designed to confuse the U-Boats of our location. When a change was required the Commodore would give us instructions to follow, allowing for what should be a seamless diversion. When setting off, a ship would be given instructions about how many degrees they were to travel and in what direction, e.g. x degrees north to starboard. The entire convoy would all be steering this established course and at a given flag and sound signal the entire convoy would alter course, holding this course until the next order. Orders were given using flag signals and every ship in the convoy would see the signal. The drill was that all the ships then responded to the signal by hoisting an answering pennant. It was here that things got messy – mistakes were often made. This was because the Radios Officers on Merchant ships were often not fully trained, and lacked the experience of the Commodore's staff who were Royal Navy men. Keeping station in a convoy required considerable skill and vigilance on the part of the navigating crew. Although the radio officers went on bridge watch they also had specific radio listening duties, recording the Admiralty instructions which were coming over the wireless. The multi-tasking meant that flag and Aldis Lamp signalling skills were often not of a particularly high standard.

There was one memorable occasion which illustrated this point admirably. I went on bridge watch and took a flag signal from the Commodore. I duly noted the message and passed it onto the Navigating Officer. I then had to raise the answering pennant but this pennant was not in the usual pigeon hole on the bridge, and we started a panic search for it. Eventually, in exasperation, the Chief Officer told us he would go down below deck and bring out the spare flag. I turned round to watch him go and for no apparent reason I looked up at the yardarm. To my horror I saw the answering pennant fluttering away up there. It had been left there since the previous message. The criticism of the Merchant Navy signallers had some justification and we were duly mortified as we lowered the pennant and then, after a respectful pause, raised it again. Even if the message was received and acted upon by all the ships, there remained more – almost insurmountable – problems to overcome to ensure all the ships steered the same course, at the same time. We were a motley collection of Merchant ships all built to different designs and specifications: steam; oil and diesel. Each ship was a different size – from a small tramp steamer to the mighty passenger liner. Although every ship turned its steering mechanism to the same number of degrees each ship responded to that diversion very differently. Turning circles all took place in dangerously close formation. It was like the dodgem cars. Not only did these manoeuvres require the skill of the helmsman and navigating officers but it also stretched the patience and ingenuity of the engineering crew and the firemen on the coal burners. These manoeuvres may not have always confused the submarine commanders but it certainly confused some of the Merchant personnel.

The convoy split as it passed Gibraltar. The Holmbury went into the Mediterranean and the rest of the ships sailed to South Africa. Once through the Gibraltar Strait we edged into the neutral waters at Melilla Harbour. We were not allowed ashore and by the same token only specified visitors were allowed on board. The climate in the region was quite pleasant at that time of year, and I was eager to get to Gibraltar. We elbowed our way into Gibraltar around Europa Point[18] but gave the Spanish port of Algeciras[19] a wide berth. As a British territory, Gibraltar was home to both a naval and air base. It was like a fortress with the Army, Navy and Air Force all present. It was of course protected by booms, and it had not yet experienced the novel and daring Italian 'one man Subs'[20]. These caused a lot of bother until a defence was mastered.[21] Approaching the Spanish coast, the lights of the mainland caused me to yearn after peacetime. I resented the Spanish for being able to live in such a care free manner, at such ease. They could

---

[18] Europa Point is the most southerly point of Gibraltar. On a clear day, one can see North Africa from it.

[19] As one of the largest ports in Europe, Algeciras is a major international port in the south west of Spain

[20] Otherwise known as a 'midget submarine' – any sub under 150 tons with a crew from anywhere from 1 to 8. Were carried by mother ships and dispensed.

[21] Defeat of said submarines would have been complete around about the time the Battle of Atlantic turned in the Allies' favour and the infamous Wolfpacks fell ineffective

put their lights on when they liked – something so simple, yet this was an impossibility for a seaman. Furthermore, it was impossible for many back in Britain. At Gibraltar we were herded into an assembly area and only the Captain and the Chief Radio Officer went ashore, attending a Commodore's meeting. The airport runway was being extended into the sea to make it long enough for larger planes and the Spanish labour force from La Linea, who were daytime visitors. Any political difficulties and reservations between Franco and the British government were inevitably diluted by a regular hard currency wage for Spanish citizens. We left Gibraltar harbour at very short notice, thus making it harder for U-Boats to be alerted to our presence in the port. We headed north briefly before diverting to the neutral waters around Lisbon. Although the Holmbury was now totally independent none of us anticipated any trouble in the waters surrounding Lisbon. That area was used as much by the enemy as it was by the allies.

Stopping at Lisbon was not what I had expected. There were no apparent restrictions on the locals coming aboard and we were free to go as we pleased. The locals who came on to our decks were eager and willing to sell us anything they thought we would buy. In this respect I saw a strange similarity between the Portuguese and the Ghanaians in what was the Gold Coast. However, in the Gold Coast the only postcards we could buy were from the Methodist Mission and depicted children at school or fishermen at work. In Lisbon the postcard seller over-zealously bounded onto the ship. He openly displayed postcards which pictured the historic sites of Lisbon, but this was just a front for a selection of 'dirty pictures.' This was standard produce in those days and would now be regarded as pornography. For reasons which I cannot begin to explain I was completely unmoved by his sales technique and, in a juvenile and mischievous mood, I bought his entire supply of cover postcards depicting the sites of Lisbon. This was much to the amusement of my fellow officers. The Foreign Office and their strictures seemed rather remote and the idea of going ashore in a peacetime city was like embarking on a mission to find the Holy Grail. However, we all agreed that we would go ashore as a group and stay together. For an entire crew to stay together when ashore was highly unusual, but we all recognised the need for it. It did not come as any surprise to learn that the first place to be visited would be a pub of some description. I remember that the beer was a light ale which suited me but brought some complaints from the seasoned drinkers. There really was no debate or vote on where we went next, the more vociferous just took it for granted that the next appetite to be assuaged was sex and we all ended up in a local brothel. The Madam running the outfit was obviously used to the rule of servicemen 'keeping in a group' and was not apparently perturbed by the fact that the horde of potential customers produced only a few actual fee paying clients. For those of us not using the brothel for its intended commercial service, we drank their beer, smoked our cigarettes and grew increasingly bored. Alcohol took its toll and eventually enough of us grouped together and returned to the ship.

The next day I awoke to a bright sun and the refreshing sound of calm, splashing waves outside. I decided to go ashore by myself and discussed it with some of the others over breakfast. One of my crew members, an engineer, seemed genuinely concerned at the idea of me wandering the streets of Lisbon on my own. Perhaps he had visions of me being set upon by a group of Portuguese spies, those more willing and able to use violence as a form of coercion. As I left the saloon he quietly handed me his revolver and bullets. I did not want his gun but at the same time I was just a boy who did not want to offend any of my fellow crewmen. So I took the revolver after receiving some basic instructions as to how it worked. I spent a day in Lisbon in awe of the shops, full of luxurious and exquisite goods. The Baroque architecture was so different from the Georgian and neo-classical style of Edinburgh. I saw the Black Horse Square, the Ajuda Palace and the impressive Municipal Buildings along with the inevitable variety of churches. I came back on board full of praise for the city and that evening, over dinner, easily convinced some of the men to join me the following day. We went to Estoril and marvelled at the famous hotel.[22] It had the sparkle and magic of a hotel whipped straight from a film set. We then explored the coastline and its variety of seafood restaurants. I was seeing and eating fish that I had never heard of and it was totally enchanting. I felt like I had been transported to some new fantasy land. I was

---

[22] A town in the Municipality of Cascais, in the district of Lisbon. The town is famous for its beautiful beaches and stunning architecture.

Alice, wandering through my very own Wonderland and it was dazzling. We swam in the Tagus, the pleasant spring sunshine warming up our backs. The only thing to spoil this otherwise perfect afternoon was the slimy sludge on the riverbed. Some of us were then invited out by a few pro-British local residents. They took us to their wine cellars and presented us with a variety of different wines. I had not yet acquired a taste for wine and didn't fully appreciate the generosity of their gifts, but sipping on the refreshing beverage was nonetheless a treat. We were in Lisbon for four days and it floated by like a thoroughly enjoyable and vivid dream. The only thing which irritated me was being constantly pestered by some of the locals to give them information about our life at sea and at home. They were presumably hoping that we would provide them with information they could sell to the Germans.

As the four day stopover in Lisbon came to a close, a few of us gathered at the dockside to bid our farewells to the city. A local photographer appeared and persuaded us to have our photograph taken. He manoeuvred us into order and was careful to ensure that the stern of the ship was in shot, thereby displaying the Holmbury's mounted gun. The weapon was given pride of place in his photograph. We left Lisbon on 11th February and reached South Wales in early March. It's an indication of the devious and tactical route which we had to take, that it took us almost a month to sail back to Britain. We waited until there was a northbound convoy passing by which we could latch on to, providing us with some necessary protection. Despite these tedious precautions (which were effective) we arrived in the Bristol Channel with a safe and secure full cargo. Our iron ore was delivered to the hungry iron foundries of Port Talbot.

On March 7th we arrived in Cardiff, where we were to be signed off. Entering the nearest bar, I settled down for a beer with a few of my fellow seamen. The first round was on me and I gallantly strolled up to the bar. After being signed off from the Holmbury by the Ministry of Shipping, the radio officers were to report to the nearby Marconi offices.[23] There, I was given 14 days leave and a travel pass to Edinburgh.

---

[23] Marconi were a worldwide quasi-government organisation. Their offices, located around the UK, were used for official business during the war.

5 – 1942: On thin ice?

The initial months of 1942 are a crucial moment in modern British history. For the British, victory seemed unlikely. It tipped favourably towards the Germans. 1941 had left Britain battered and bruised. In that year the 'Blitz' had officially concluded, starting in September 1940 and coming to its first *major* end in May 1941. Approximately 74,000 tons of bombs were dropped on Britain in that time. Britain had avoided a feared German invasion and occupation, unlike many of her neighbours. However, this apparent success was more the result of Britain's geographical positioning rather than the efforts of the RAF alone. Being an island nation she was hard to reach, and surrounded by shallow waters, it was virtually impossible for German trawlers to land troops. An amphibious attack, realistically, could not have occurred.[24] By March 1942, British bases in the East had been lost. Hong Kong fell to the Japanese on Christmas Day 1941. After three weeks, on 15th February 1942, Commonwealth forces surrendered Singapore to the Japanese. Churchill described the

---

[24] The Royal Navy and Coastal Command did protect the Channel, with Coastal Command bombing 19 German ships in the Channel in September 1941 alone. This point should not be discounted, even if the fundamental reason which ultimately prevented a German invasion was the inability to access British shores for geographical reasons.

loss of Singapore as 'the worst disaster and largest capitulation in British history'. His memoirs detail the 'direct shock' of receiving the news. He expressed relief at being alone when the call arrived. The loss of Hong Kong and Singapore resulted in approximately 62,000 prisoners of war. By spring 1942 the British war momentum was flagging and the ever-diminishing Empire growing increasingly fragile.

Efforts in the North Atlantic proved similarly troublesome. For any country to win a war, it must first provide for itself. This was strongly felt in Britain: the North Atlantic was fundamental to the war effort. Britain could not be totally self-sufficient. Being an island nation may have been advantageous in that invasion became a far off possibility, but it forced Britain to rely heavily on the Merchant Navy for vital resources. Half of all food and two thirds of other resources passed through the Atlantic to get to Britain during the war. The period between June 1940 and early 1943 went through two phases of what German U-Boat officers called their 'happy time'. The German occupation of France allowed them to form invaluable U-Boat bases on the west coast, a perfect launching pad for the Atlantic. Admiral Doenitz, the commander of the Kriegsmarine's U-Boat fleet, had studied the convoy system during the Great War. Educated in how to wound and destabilise Allied convoy systems, he ordered his submarines to attack in packs of approximately a dozen; named Wolf Packs. Individual submarines might spot a ship or convoy and manage to fire a few hits, with perhaps one successful hit, before having to escape. But gangs of U-Boats were

The Memoirs of Alfred Hodgson

highly efficient, with safety in numbers. Doenitz ensured that the U-Boats could communicate with nearby submarines and the headquarters at St Lorient. This allowed them to group together, stalking a convoy until they were ready to attack. Doenitz also quickly learned that the ASDIC detection system installed on British ships could not detect surface vessels. Therefore, he bypassed the system by informing his U-Boats to lie in shallow water at night. This way, they were undetectable by the naked eye and impenetrable by ASDIC. During the so-called 'happy time' an average of 920 tons of British supplies were lost daily. An estimated 62 million tonnes of Allied shipping was destroyed in the North Atlantic in 1942. By the end of the year Britain sat close to running out of oil. It was a battle of attrition.

Britain started 1942 in a less than positive position. On-going bombings ravaged many parts of the home front whilst the Merchant Navy was crippled by advancing submarines in the Atlantic. But one land victory in the winter of 1942 marks a change of fate, and the beginning of significant advances for the Allied armies. Montgomery's victory in El Alamein in November 1942 proved hugely important, arguably defining the close of the year and setting up 1943 in a more optimistic light. Off of the thin ice and onto solid ground. The First Battle of El Alamein occurred in July 1942, resulting in a triumphant victory for the German Panzers. However, the British and Commonwealth Army would go on to have one hugely important, and influential, victory a mere four months later. General Montgomery led the 8th British

Edited by Katherine Hodgson

Army to a firm defeat of General Rommel's Panzers, forcing them out of Libya and into Tunisia.[25] Montgomery made efficient use of the air force for overhead support. The Desert Rats bombed the German supply lines and helped break down their defensive lines. On 23rd October Montgomery combined air and ground weapons to lead his force to victory. He received widespread recognition as one of the war's finest generals, with renowned military historian John Keegan noting: 'Montgomery's debut on the battlefield had been one of the most brilliant in the history of Generalship.'[26]

The 1st November 1942 saw Allied armoured divisions breaking through the German defensive lines. These lines were nicknamed the 'Devil's Garden' by German troops, believed to be impenetrable. It was on this date that Rommel ran out of petrol. The following day, the Desert Fox messaged Hitler explain his troops would be 'annihilated' if they stayed any longer. This same message was intercepted by British intelligence. Montgomery held the intercepted message in his hand as the last of

---

[25] General Erwin Rommel, nicknamed the Desert Fox, was a highly respected German field marshal. Skilled at getting his troops to attack from the front rather than the rear, Rommel had a long successful infantry career. In 1940 he was appointed Commander of the 7th Panzer Division. In 1941 he was promoted to General of the Afrika Korps and for a while led a highly successful North African campaign. Rommel was involved in a plot to overthrow and kill Hitler, when this was uncovered he took his own life in 1944.

[26] C.F. Baxter, 'Field Marshal Bernard Law Montgomery, 1887-1976: A Selected Bibliography,' (Greenwood, 1999) p.3

Rommel's Panzers retreated to Tunisia on 4th November. Twenty five thousands Germans and Italians had been killed or wounded in the battle and 13,000 Allied troops in the 8th Army. El Alamein signalled new found confidence for the British military. It was the first significant *land* battle for the British Army, leading the way for more to come. It is therefore not surprising that Churchill uttered the famous words, 'before Alamein, we never had a victory. After Alamein, we never had a defeat.'

The Second Battle of El Alamein marked Allied supremacy in North Africa. It was the first and only ground battle won by the British and Commonwealth Armies without the direct involvement of the US Army. It occurred in a year of allied troubles: of defeats in the North Atlantic; of a home front still struggling with poverty and rationing, trying to recover from the greatest sustained period of Luftwaffe bombings the war would bring. It occurred in a year when the Eastern Empire diminished, and when US aid and military support was being increasingly relied upon. In the closing months of 1942 Britain threw a crucial blow against the German Army, defeating one of their most respected and feared generals. Gaining control in North Africa proved to be strategically important. Allied forces now controlled the Western Desert in North Africa and the Suez Canal. A highly important turn of events was about to occur, with a Russian victory at Stalingrad. Then, in May 1943 the Axis forces left North Africa for good. Things were looking up.

Following a Nazi invasion, the Soviets switched to the Allied side. Operation Barbarossa[27] began in June 1941 and catapulted the two dictatorships into a vicious land battle in the east, lasting four years. The Battle of Stalingrad stretched from August 1942 to February 1943. Stalingrad was crucial. It was a battle which heavily engaged the Nazis; forcing them to concentrate vast amounts of land and air power to the eastern front. In turn, Nazis forces in the west were left vulnerable. Stalingrad can be seen as 'the turning point of the *war*.'[28] The destruction of the German 6th Army marked a momentous change in the war's course. From his cell at the Nuremberg Trials, Ribbentrop noted the three reasons for the Nazi's defeat: the might and the persistence of the Red Army; US Lend Lease; and the Allied bombing campaign. The Allied victory in Eastern Europe substantiates his first two points.

That being said, the success of the Russian Army depended heavily on financial aid from elsewhere – as Ribbentrop noted. The USA and Britain produced and lent tonnes of machinery to the USSR during their eastern campaign. This was most notable in 1941 and 1942. Britain declared 22nd September 1941 'Tanks for Russia Day.' Every piece of weaponry manufactured in those 24 hours was shipped straight to Arkhangelsk (Archangel), via dangerous Arctic

---

[27] 3 million German troops invaded Russia on 22 June 1941.
[28] Richard Overy: original quote is, 'Some historians have seen this as the turning point of the war.'
'The Soviet-German War 1941-1945', BBC History, (2011) Italics my own.

convoy routes. By the end of September 1941, 450 aircraft and 22k tons of rubber had been given to Stalin. The end of 1941 also witnessed Stalin welcoming aid from the Americans. Correlli Barnett describes Lend Lease as an 'American life support machine'[29] for Britain, but it was equally as important to the Soviets. Without such material and economic support success in the east would have been unachievable.

The victory of the Russian Army in 1943 was a catalyst for the Allied victory two years later. The victory at Stalingrad is vitally important to the Allied campaign and war momentum. Its very existence highlights the danger of 1942. But its success also highlights the growing strength of the Allies. A strength dependent on a powerful Russian land army, which in turn weakened the German one. And it was a strength reflected in the British Army by the end of 1942. But most importantly, it was a strength reliant on the financial support of the USA.

1942 was undoubtedly a mixed bag. It witnessed significant defeats to the allied forces, whether that be on land or at sea. But there was also notable victories, albeit in the closing months of the year. El Alamein was the first of many crucial victories for the allies. It was, one might say, a precursor to the larger victories of 1943: the victory at Stalingrad a few short months later; allied supremacy in the North Atlantic being solidified in the spring of 1943; and further Russian

---

[29] C. Barnett 'The Lost Victory: British Dreams, British Realities 1945-1950', Faber Finds, (1995).

victories in summer 1943. 1942 began catastrophically for the Allies. But it was not a year entirely at loss. Financial aid from the Americans began to take shape. And fortunes slowly began to turn. 1942 contains important events. It contains important victories. The Allies may have been on thin ice for the most 1942, but it was a year when they grew in strength and the Germans weakened. Victories in 1943 only serve to further highlight that.

6 – *The Third Voyage: Into the Breach*

SS Delillian: completed in 1923 this 6,423 ton steam ship was owned by Donaldson Brothers Ltd, Glasgow. Its homeport was in Liverpool and the vessel survived the entirety of the war. It was torpedoed and damaged on 7th March 1941 by the U-70. Of the 68 man crew, all survived. The ship returned to Port Glasgow to undergo repairs and was resumed service in May 1941. After the war the Delillian was broken up at Port Glasgow in February 1954.

Edited by Katherine Hodgson

I arrived home on St. Patrick's Day 1942. I was due 14 days leave and was excited to spend it with my family. Despite my mother being Irish we did little to celebrate the feast of St Patrick. Edinburgh as a whole did little. It would have been acknowledged by the priest the following Sunday, but aside from that slight nod to the Patron Saint of Ireland, the predominantly Presbyterian capital barely took any notice of the festivity. My mother did, however, wear a shamrock as a sign of national pride and saintly devotion. Even if we had been accustomed to celebrating every March in a grand and loud fashion, with the best will in the world, it would have been totally impossible to celebrate in the throngs of war.

I was sent to Liverpool to join the SS Delillian on 2nd April 1942. I soon received word that my next voyage would be to Canada to load up with munitions. This made me feel very apprehensive as it was a particularly unhealthy cargo to be carrying at this stage in the war, especially across the unpleasant Mid Atlantic Gap. The convoy left Liverpool in a very orderly fashion and was well protected by a variety of naval escorts and aircraft. We had a *Short Sunderland Flying Boat*[30] hovering overhead like a mother duck

---

[30] A high quality military flying boat patrol bomber, the Sunderland was manufactured by the Short Brothers and formally introduced in 1938. It was created for the RAF but became one of the most widely used flying boats in the war. The RAF continued to use the Sunderlands until 1959, and they played a part in the Korean War. A flying boat is a seaplane with a hull. A patrol bomber is air bound naval reconnaissance.

and *Hudson* aircraft also in support.[31] As we reached the mid-Atlantic the convoy faded, the smaller Naval escorts returned to the UK for refuelling while the aircraft returned to base having reached their operational range. At this point, only two escort vessels could be spotted from the decks of the Delillian. This was a harrowing sight – to look out and see bare, vast stretches of water for miles. Despite this we were assured that there was another vessel over the horizon but that sinking feeling of isolation didn't pass easily. We were virtually on our own with hordes of Wolf Packs roaming the Atlantic, hunting us down. Self-preservation was essential and the Commodore did his level best to maintain a safe journey. We changed course, zig-zagged, twisted and turned. These constant course diversions certainly confused any trailing submarine but it also inadvertently confused our navigation officers who struggled to establish our position. The weather was poor, the skies filled with thick clouds. This meant neither the sun nor stars were visible so our position had to be established by 'dead reckoning.'[32] Such rough guide navigation is

---

[31] The Lockheed Husdon Patrol Bomber was used by the RAF as a bomber, reconnaissance aircraft and a maritime patrol craft. It was a converted civil aircraft which began operational service with the RAF in the summer of 1939. At its peak there were 17 Hudson squadrons. By early 1940 the Hudsons received ASV radar and were heavily used in supporting convoys across the Atlantic, starting from August 1940. The US Navy and Air force used Hudsons also.

[32] A form of sheer navigational guess work. Officers would have tried to calculate their location by working back from when they could last definitely establish their whereabouts. This quasi-scientific attempt at locating the ship would have been very

acceptable when you are surrounded by only the bare ocean but is problematic in the confines of a convoy. Every day at noon the navigation officers assembled on the bridge, hoping for a break in the cloud cover. These daily meetings would be followed by a flurry of Aldis signals, comparing notes with our neighbouring ships. It was a navigational mess which we could have done without.

One morning, to our delight and virtual disbelief, off the starboard bow a line of Canadian warships appeared under the hazy pink sun. We were headed for St. John's[33] and the news soon reached us that U-Boats had penetrated the St Lawrence[34] and sunk three allied ships. To combat this, the Canadian Navy and Air Force blanketed the St. Lawrence. This was good news for us, creating a solid level of protection. St. John's was a convoy assembly area and a safe haven for us; it was here that we learned that we could not immediately proceed up the St. Lawrence River (as planned) because the surface was frozen over with ice. To temporarily remove us from the harsh reality of naval warfare, we prepared to be part of the annual race up the St Lawrence to Quebec. The race was to take place as soon as the ice began to melt and was a

---

difficult to do and required the ability to guess distances, speeds, wind and currents etc. accurately.

[33] Located on the eastern tip of the Avalon Peninsula (in the island of Newfoundland), St John's is the largest and capital city of Newfoundland, Canada. During the war St John's acted as a base for the British and Canadian navies. There was also an American Air Force base called Fort Peppernell in the city.

[34] The St Lawrence is a large Canadian river flowing south-west to north-east and crossing the provinces of Quebec and Ontario.

novel event, able to fire the imagination. The rules were well established: we had to anchor at the mouth of the river and await the signal that the ice had broken. A specific route was set and we could not cut corners; then, the race began. The first ship to Quebec was the winner. I do not remember how many ships were waiting to start but there was one other serious contender who we watched carefully. We got some advance warning that the ice was breaking and the engineers gave us a full head of steam in preparation for setting off. As a coal burning ship; the Delillian's firemen had to work like demons to ensure a sufficient speed. Firemen on board were usually Irish or Lascar seamen[35], both of which had a reputation for being highly skilled and hard working. There was a high mortality rate for these men and often the Indian lascars had no fingertips, due to the risks involved with working as a fireman. For reasons completely unknown we won, entering Quebec as champions. On arrival the Mayor of Quebec greeted us with a civic reception. I have only a vague memory of the celebratory events but the Captain was given a silver topped cane and an almighty applause. All the officers received a gift and mine was an elaborate leather belt

---

[35] Seamen from the Indian Subcontinent employed to serve on European ships. Such employment had occurred since the 16th century and involved men from Eastern Asia, the Caribbean and Africa. The Merchant Navy relied heavily on such men, particularly in 1941 and '43 when they were shortages of European seamen. The Lascars also worked as cooks and stewards. Pay and conditions on board for many lascars were poor and many lascars are recorded as having demanded better standards on several occasions.

which I kept for many years. The firemen, who arguably worked the hardest to achieve our victory, were never acknowledged. I found this particularly uncomfortable and completely unfair.

Once the frivolities in Quebec had passed, I took time off to visit Montreal. I met up with one of the clerkesses I had worked with in Howden and Molleson. It was a brief, one day tour of the new and modern city. Unlike Edinburgh, steeped in rich heritage and historic buildings, Montreal was a rapidly developing cosmopolitan city with a strong French influence and allegiance. My day trip was a welcomed respite before I returned to the Delillian. From Quebec we sailed back to St John's and joined the convoy back to Britain.

On the return journey we were supported by some British corvettes and the Canadian Navy. It was a fast convoy comprised of steamships and motor vessels. We sailed at an average of 12-14 knots. One of the problems with fast convoys was that the slower ships generally struggled to maintain the average speed. These ships were known as the 'stragglers' and although frequently harried and chivvied by the escorts they inevitably failed to maintain the speed required and fell back. As a coal burning ship, the Delillian could mostly adapt to any speed by controlling the steam pressure, but the convoy contained some oil burning vessels which were plagued by the basic problem of vibration. These ships had what they called a 'vibration speed'[36] and as luck would have it, the convoy speed was often within their range of vibration speeds. This proved problematic for these ships as a vibrating engine could cause some significant damage. A further group of ships always caused some disquiet – the neutral ships. They often joined the convoy and fell back when it became dark, they would then catch up in daylight. There could be a perfectly good reason for this behaviour but unproven rumours did float about. People murmured and claimed the neutral ships fell back to rendezvous with the U-Boats and reveal the status of the convoy. It was standard practice for some neutral ships to join the convoy. The official response for this was that the neutral ships had requested the protection of the convoy.

Our return trip was peppered with alerts, depth-charge attacks and diversions. Many of the diversions were so erratic that we sailed close to Greenland and Iceland. Consequently, we endured freezing conditions on the northern end of our route. The Delillian had an open bridge so seeking shelter from the sharp Arctic breeze was not easy and the discomfort was acute. It was a tradition on British ships to not use external heaters to keep the deck warm. The theory behind it was that if it was too warm on deck the seamen would become drowsy. However, if it was kept bitterly cold they would remain sharp and alert. To compensate for a lack of heat the Navy used 'Dodgers' to divert the cold winds

---

[36] Every engine is susceptible to vibration. To control the vibration, speed is either decreased or increased.

from the deck. The Dodger was a strip of canvas, about 8cm deep, which could be rolled out and fixed to the top of the forward deck at chin level. When you stood close to the canvas it diverted the cold wind up above you without obstructing your view of the sea. Certainly, it obstructed your immediate view of the deck but this was deemed an acceptable risk to take.

Passing by Iceland created a sense of relief. It was an air base for both the British, US and Canadian Air Forces and air cover became a very real form of protection in clear weather. If the water was clear the planes could spot the submarines underwater and give away their position. This was a very effective deterrent to marauding U-Boats. It was unfortunate that poor weather meant that aircraft was frequently unable to carry out this vital task. It was, instead, the combined efforts of both the Canadian escorts and air cover which guided us safely back to Liverpool.

Walking onto land at the busy decks in Liverpool, I promised myself I would cherish my next leave. All five, short days of leave. But they were my five days.

7 – The Fourth Voyage: From Cape Race to 'Cape Fear'

<u>SS Cape Race:</u> a steam ship weighing 3807 tons. Completed in 1930, it was originally named the *Knight of St John*. In 1934 it was bought by the Lyle Shipping Co. Ltd, Glasgow and renamed. Cape Race sank in the mid-Atlantic on 10th August 1942 by the U-660. Of the 63 on board, everyone survived. Its cargo of 3979 tons of timber and 1040 tons of steel was lost.

Edited by Katherine Hodgson

June typically marks the start of summer in Britain. Sitting in my back garden, reading the morning paper, the first of the summer sun glowed down upon me. I sipped my tea and flicked through the broadsheet pages, skimming past the multiple stories centred on the war and instead concentrating intensely on the sports results, and local marriage and birth listings. I wanted something – anything – to nullify my mind from the ever present war and the destruction it brought with it. My time off meant I had to disassociate myself from the fight. Work life and home life absolutely could not co-exist, and if that meant not even reading about how my colleagues fared, then so be it. As I read the last of the football results, my mother sat down beside me.

'Good morning.' She said, handing me a telegram. It was notification of my next voyage. I was to join the SS Cape Race in Glasgow, setting sail on June 6th for the USA. Our first stop was Boston, Massachusetts. I was terribly excited at the prospect of going to the USA.

The trip out was relatively calm. We were going out 'light under ballast' – meaning the ship had no cargo and was effectively empty. Without a load, a ship will be top heavy and unstable. To try and balance the Cape Race we put some cobblestones at the bottom. Being so light, the ship could travel at its maximum speed and combined with the skill and effort of the Irish firemen on board, the Cape Race had no difficulty in keeping up with the fast convoy she had joined. The Irish firemen were always welcomed on board because they took a pride in being able to

The Memoirs of Alfred Hodgson

keep a head of steam at all times, regardless of the weather or the working conditions. They were never interested in the amount of smoke they produced when drawing the fires. The Commodores were forever messaging us to tell us to reduce the smoke because it could easily give away the position of the convoy. We had the inevitable alarms on the outward journey – the zig zags, depth charges and course diversions. They had all become part and parcel of the job.

On arrival in Boston my first surprise was meeting the *Pinkerton Men*.[37] They were responsible for the security of the ship and established, with ourselves, an anti-sabotage watch rota. The entire crew had to participate, with the exception of the firemen who worked themselves to a standstill while at sea and would go ashore and get drunk when they landed. The Pinkerton Men gave us a briefing – detailing how to act appropriately in the USA. The first lesson was about our interaction with the police force. The American police would guide us and look after us if we put ourselves in their care. They could obtain for us fantastic discounts in many of the local shops. I had a big shopping list for my family: confectionary; clothes; ornaments and a china 42- piece tea set, which took pride of place at the top of my long list.

---

[37] The Pinkerton Agency is a worldwide corporate risk management firm. It was founded in 1850 as the Pinkerton Detective Agency by Scottish immigrant Allan Pinkerton, Chicago's first police detective. The Pinkerton detectives assisted the police in catching criminals and preventing crime throughout the USA. By 1930 Allan Pinkerton's great grandson, Robert Pinkerton was in charge and the armed investigators provided security to allied ships as one of many jobs.

This was a luxury item and one I was looking forward to buying. A Boston policeman escorted me round the shops to buy everything I wanted and then led me back to the ship. Trudging back to my cabin, with my arms wrapped around several heaving bags, one of the Pinkerton detectives stopped me. 'Need a hand?' he asked, grabbing the tea set from my hand and into his own.

Thanking him I began to excitedly tell him about the numerous discounts I had received. 'It's so generous of the police to help us like that.'

The detective smirked, 'They get paid commission from all the shops you've bought from.' Not so generous after all but one clever marketing ploy.

A few days later I reluctantly hailed down a Yellow Cab. The policeman had advised me never to take a Yellow Cab as they would cheat me, always take a Blue Cab. Failing to find a Blue Cab, I opted for its feared yellow counterpart instead. To my surprise they charged the same as the Blue Cab and also gave me a detailed receipt. On recounting this story to the Pinkerton detective he explained, with a muffled laugh, that the policeman would get a commission from the Blue Cab Company also.

After collecting the load in Boston, we sailed through the Cape Cod Canal to avoid U-Boats positioned on the coastline. We were travelling to Providence, Rhode Island.[38] The ship was to remain in

---

[38] An artificial water way in Massachusetts which connects Cape Cod Bay to Buzzards Bay.

Providence for a few days so I decided to take a train into New York to see the famed concrete jungle. A city I had always wished to visit. Sitting on the train in, I fantasized about walking into Grand Central Station, with its gleaming marble facades, and strolling out into the busy streets crammed full of pedestrians, yellow taxis and towering skyscrapers. It was a buzzing metropolis I had only ever glimpsed through the medium of a camera and one which I hoped would live up to my high expectations. The train to New York was frequent and inexpensive. The majority of passengers were male and I was intrigued by the way they all sat down in silence, kept their hats on and became totally absorbed in their newspapers. The ticket collector trundled along and I was surprised to see that the men just ignored him, engrossed in the Dow Jones and football results. The few women on the train politely offered their tickets for inspection. At first, I presumed that this behaviour might be some bizarre gender preference ritual until I realised that the men stuck their tickets into their hatbands (and since this was an apparently established custom), the ticket collector just helped himself to the tickets from each hatband. Dismounting the train and exiting the impressive Grand Central Station, I stumbled out onto wild, bustling streets. It was the most vibrant and cosmopolitan place I had ever been. I was pushed and shoved through the throngs of manic pedestrians, who charged and thundered along the pavements and into shops, cafes, apartment blocks and offices. It was a warm, pleasant day and I explored the city centre at my leisure. By mid-afternoon I stopped for a cup of tea in the cafe at the Radio City Music Hall. I had always been aware that the Americans did not like tea and I was now to learn why. As far as the waitress was concerned my request was duly satisfied by handing me a cup of hot water, followed a few minutes later, by placing a teabag in front of me. Presumably I had to dip it into the cup of now lukewarm water. Needless to say the drink was not a success. That evening I acquainted myself with the Gordon family. They lived in a comfortable apartment in the Bronx and were relatives of close friends of mine from Edinburgh. On learning that I would be travelling to the USA, I had been given the family's contact details and had arranged to visit them. I stayed in their home for two nights and was treated to fine food, wine and plenty of entertainment. This brief stopover in New York City exposed me to their everyday life. Their household appliances were all brand new and top of the range. Everything we had in east coast Scotland they had in east coast America but upgraded. My second day in New York entailed a leisurely stroll through Central Park with Mr and Mrs Gordon's daughter, who was roughly the same age as me. We passed a small group of rowdy, jeering men. I did not hear properly what they were yelling but she did and it upset her to the point of making an issue out of it. I persuaded her to let it go, it was not worth bothering about. It later transpired that the group of men had shouted abuse at the potential sight of 'Limey'[39]

---

[39] A derogatory nickname used for British citizens. It was specifically accredited to British seamen because in the years before ships had refrigerators, seamen would frequently suffer ailments and illnesses as the result of poor quality food. To

personnel in uniform taking 'the girls away from the local menfolk'.

I returned to Providence first thing the following morning. The Cape Race glided up to Sydney, Nova Scotia where we were to meet the convoy SC-94 on 5th August.[40] The SC-94 was destined for Liverpool and under the protection of the Cl escort group.[41] This was an efficient and reliable escort group which I was thankful to have close by. Despite this reinforcement, a thick and heavy fog dominated the first few days of the journey and for the most part we were unable to see our escorts from the deck. Within the convoy, the ships used horns to alert each other of their positions. This was particularly unsettling because despite having the sound of the horn beckoning towards you, the fog still made it difficult to judge distance and pinpoint exactly where the sound had originated from. On 5th August the first ship in the convoy was sunk. It was one of eight romped vessels which had formed a small splinter group behind the SC-94.[42] The U-593 sank the Dutch Merchant steam ship, *Spar* which had been previously spotted along with seven more ships

---

counteract this, they drank lime juice and ate limes to try and stay healthy.

[40] Sydney is on Cape Breton Island in the Province of Nova Scotia in north east Canada.

[41] Was an Anglo-Canadian escort group consisting of the British corvettes Nasturtium, Dianthus and Primrose. There were also two Canadian corvettes – the Chilliwack and Orilllia and the Canadian Destroyers HMCS Battleford and HMCS Assiniboine.

[42] Six Merchant ships and two escorts had splintered from the main body of the convoy on August 3rd. They had failed to realise that there was a course diversion due to the fog.

by the aforementioned submarine. [43] The U-593 was one of nine outbound submarines that assisted eight of the submarines from the Steinbrinck Wolfpack.[44] The first eight U-Boats were behind us and nine approached from the front. It would be this combined group of seventeen vessels which would lead the SC-94 to an explosive and brutal five days of naval warfare. This resulted in the sinking of 11 ships and 2 U-Boats, along with the deaths of 54 allied and 46 German seamen.

We altered our course after the Spar's sinking and immediately ran into further fog. This time it was a freezing fog. Certainly, the heavy fog gave a degree of protection but it was hazardous to sail in, unpleasant and uncomfortable. The fog lasted two days and it was extremely nerve-wracking with ships frequently emerging from the fog and just missing the Cape Race's paintwork. When the fog cleared we were in a different world: no longer were there 35 ships floating among one and other, but rather bare stretches of quiet sea. It was as if we had all been dropped into a colander, shaken and then dropped out again. The escorts' first task was to round up all the ships and pull them back together.

---

[43] The Spar had been one of the eight disbanded vessels. At 18.48 on 5th August the U-593 fired three torpedoes at three of the group but the Spar was the only one to be hit.
[44] Contained 8 submarines – the U-210, U-379, U-454, U-607 and U-704. They would later be joined by nine outbound submarines – U-176, U-174, U-256, U-438, U-595, U-605, U-660 and U-705.

The initial skirmish occurred on 5th August but the vast majority of damage ensued between 8th and 10th. On 6th August the U-210[45] was sunk just south of Greenland by HMCS Assiniboine using a combination of ramming, gunfire and depth charges. It would not be until 1pm on 8th that the attacking Wolfpack would *successfully* strike again. The British steam ship, the Anneberg and the American steam ship, the Kaimoku, were the first casualties followed by the British vessel, Kelso, shortly afterwards.[46] Following the loss of these three Merchant ships, the U-379 was sunk by a cocktail of ramming and depth charges, at the hands of *HMS Dianthus.*[47] This illustrates just how effective these corvettes were: they were small; compact and very sturdy. They could survive a ramming much better than the sleek Destroyers which were built for speed and fire power but with little to no body armour.

At one point a ship close to us was attacked. The force of the explosion gave the impression that we ourselves had been hit. The engines were stopped while the Captain (Master James Barnetson) gave orders for the engineers to give a damage report. At Sydney we had picked up a group of twelve survivors from Port Nicholson, a Merchant ship which had been sunk the previous month. These twelve men had interpreted the silence from the engines as meaning the ship was sinking. They lowered a lifeboat and took off. All of a sudden the Cape Race was short one

---

[45] Six died from the complement of 43.
[46] Four were killed on the Kaimoku and three lost their lives on the Kelso.
[47] 40 died from the U-379

precious life boat for her own crew. The survivors from Port Nicholson had been jittery from the start – their nerves shattered after their experience. They didn't get far before the engineers reported that there was no apparent damage and Master Barnetson used the loud hailer to recall the lifeboat. The twelve survivors returned rather sheepishly while we joined the scatter routine.[48]

By the 8th August the Cape Race was stationed near the front of the convoy formation, a couple of rows behind the Commodore. The Commodore – Vice Admiral Dashwood Fowler Moir – was on board the *Trehata*. I was on bridge watch at around 3pm, keeping an eye out for signals from the Commodore. Suddenly, the Trehata's yardarm became obscured. I immediately presumed it was just fog but soon realised that a growing body of smoke was the culprit. The smoke grew bigger and bigger and ascended higher and higher. What then faced me was a mushroom of explosive smoke and flames. There was no sound. It was deathly quiet. I saw the explosion before I heard it. When the sound eventually did reach me it was so shattering and ear-splitting that I flung myself to the floor, clasping my hands over my ears. A baleful sob from the Trehata's horn cried out as the crew desperately tried to put out one final signal. It is a haunting noise forever lodged inside my brain. It groaned and whined just as the ship's funnel collapsed. There was no need for a signal, it was all

---

[48] This was when the Commodore gave the order for all the remaining ships in a convoy to scatter thereby confusing the U-Boats while the escorts turned their attention to a counter attack.

too clear that the Commodore was no longer in command. The Rear Commodore[49] raced up the middle of the convoy flying the Commodore's pennant and taking position at the front.[50] The following day a straggler, the *Radchurch,* sank and two men were killed.

As the attack continued into the 10th four more ships were sank. The first being the Greek Merchant ship, the *Condylis*. Nine of her crew and 6924 tons of cargo were lost. At 12.20 the U-660 was positioned starboard, south of Iceland. It fired one torpedo, which was recorded as detonating 47 seconds later, then a further two which detonated one and a half minutes after. A third detonated 50 seconds after the previous two. The U-438 also fired in a similar timeframe but from the left hand side. The Condylis was hit on both sides, therefore receiving hits from both submarines. The Cape Race sank next, being the only other ship to be hit by one of the U-660's torpedoes. The *Oregon*[51] and *Empire Reindeer* were also hit, with the former being damaged and falling behind and the latter sinking almost instantly.

I can vividly remember the long, drawn out moments before the ship disappeared into the whirlpool. This time there was no doubt that we had

---

[49] In naval convoys there would be a Commodore stationed on a ship at both the front and back of the convoy.

[50] Ships in a convoy were positioned in columns. They were identified by pennant flag number rather than name, e.g. pennant number 34 was a ship three in and in the fourth column along.

[51] The U-438 returned to the Oregon at dusk and managed to sink her then. Two people died as a consequence.

been torpedoed and the Captain gave the order to abandon ship. The well-rehearsed procedure clicked into place and I retrieved the weighted bag in which we kept the Admiralty Code Books and convoy papers. I carried them to the side of the ship and threw them over. I then collected the portable lifeboat transmitter and carried it out to the boat deck. The ship was still on a level keel so I put the transmitter into the life boat which the bridge crew would occupy, but just as I raised the almost impossible weight to shoulder level – the ship keeled over. I felt my ankle giving way but the adrenaline pumping through my body prevented me from writhing around in agony. There were far more pressing issues than a painful ankle and I hurried back to report to my senior. He told me my duties were finished and I should take to the boats. We had designated lifeboats and I headed for the boat which I was assigned to. Arriving at it I was surprised to find it deserted and empty. The Third Mate[52] (who was in charge of that lifeboat) was nearby and gave me the disturbing news that the boat could not be lowered because someone had cut the falls. There was no time to debate who had cut the falls or why, the ship was sinking and I needed to find a lifeboat. An urgent shriek from above alerted me to an approaching ship – it was thundering towards us, on a collision course. I ran to the far side and saw a lifeboat about fifteen feet below with space for at least one more and jumped.

---

[52] A navigator on the ship

Those already on the lifeboat were not too pleased at my method of arrival and any chance of preventing further damage to my ankle was lost at this point. My memory in the lifeboat is rather hazy. I remember there being a designated coxswain who gave the orders, with our main objective being to get as far away as possible from the ship and as quickly as possible. We had to avoid being sucked down by the whirlpool created when a ship sinks. These powerful currents of water would have pulled us under had we not rowed vigorously. I found myself pulling a very heavy and clumsy oar which was shared by another. The combined effort of the oars may have been successful in pulling us far enough away from the vortex but not far enough to stop us from watching the final moments of the Cape Race as its bow disappeared into the Atlantic. It took with it all of its cargo and my 42 piece tea-set. I was fairly confident everyone on board had survived, that they had enough time to seek refuge. As the ship dipped into the ocean I felt completely numb – I could not comprehend what had happened.

We then began to row away from the floating corpses and debris. We had been told that someone would come back to pick us up and we fastened onto that concept. All the lifeboats stuck together and didn't row too far from the scene of the sinking. The Cape Race went down at approximately midday. I don't remember seeing nightfall while in the lifeboat, so we can't have been shipwrecked for more than 6-8 hours. I distinctly remember hearing a loud hailer telling us to come aboard quickly as we were in dangerous waters. HMS Dianthus had arrived. They dropped scrambling nets for us. I had never used a scrambling net before and probably would have managed quite well on solid ground but the lifeboat was bucking and weaving in the North Atlantic swell. I had no difficulty in taking hold of the net but did not know the importance of getting a foothold before the swell reverted to a twenty foot drop. I was only twenty and in my prime but I felt it almost impossible to clamber up. As I reached the top some helping hands grabbed me and heaved me aboard.

'Thank you' I gasped fervently. I was in a rather dazed condition and quite happy to just collapse on the deck and lie there indefinitely. However, I was immediately invited below to join the other officers in a very crowded cabin. We were given enough to eat to stay alive and sold cigarettes. I had the sum of nine shillings and three pence deducted from my pay to meet my account at HMS Dianthus. A few hours later, the officers from the Cape Race retreated to a separate saloon where we were to sleep. It was cramped but liveable, and it was certainly more spacious than the conditions for the rest of the crew. The journey back to Liverpool lasted four days with no further alarms. The convoy had been joined by two more Destroyers on 9th August – the Blyskawica (Polish) and the Broke (British). Both of these ships had Huff Duff technology (High Frequency Direction Finder)[53] with

---

[53] A highly accurate way of detecting where U-Boats where positioned, as it picked up the high frequency radio transmitters employed on the U-Boats. Did not become commonplace on RN ships until 1942.

air cover soon arriving from Iceland. The much sought after aerial support was all too late in preventing the sinking, but returned us to Britain safely.

We landed in Liverpool on 14th August. The signing off procedure and clothing replacement was slick and my first thought when I walked ashore was to contact my uncle who lived in the city. I was welcomed with open arms by my aunt, uncle and cousin and had the unbelievable luxury of a hot, homemade meal and a bath followed by a long sleep. I contacted my parents in Edinburgh and explained what had happened but I had no great desire to travel up north or do anything. I was discharged from my service at sea once the Cape Race had sank on 10th August, and my pay from the Lyle Shipping Co. also stopped. I had 'survivors' leave' of 14 days starting from my date of return into Liverpool. Luckily for me, as a Marconi employee, there was some continuity of payment until my next signing on date. I stayed in Liverpool for a fortnight before going back home to Edinburgh.

Edited by Katherine Hodgson

8 – *The Fifth Voyage: On the Offensive*

<u>SS Reina del Pacifico:</u> built by Harland and Wolff in Belfast in 1931, the Reina was owned by the Pacific Steam Navigation Company. She was, to date, their largest steam ship and used as a passenger liner. The Reina had a gross tonnage of 17, 872 and a length of 551.3ft. In 1937 former Labour Prime Minister Ramsay Macdonald died of a heart attack aboard the Reina. She was registered and based at Liverpool and functioned as a troopship during the war. The Reina del Pacifico was involved in the landings at North Africa, Sicily and Normandy and was scrapped in 1958.

My 'survivors leave' soon passed and I left my uncle's home in Liverpool on 25th August 1942. The first few days of September were spent resting at home in Edinburgh. I filled my short, precious time in the capital drifting from one enjoyable pastime to the next: from my bedroom where I listened to music and read; to the garden where I sat chatting with family and friends. From the public library where I whittled away the hours examining the stunning architecture and immersing myself in the beautifully crafted hardbacks; to the cinema where I enjoyed a few films. The first few days in September 1942 were pleasant and tranquil but the consequences of war were felt by everyone on the home front. There was rationing, the inevitable and irritable black-outs and widespread inequality.

The worst of the Blitz had passed by 1942, but its lingering effects were still strongly felt. There exists a romantic notion that the Blitz united the British people. It certainly motivated people to defeat a common enemy, but the class system remained a stringent part of British society. Class tensions were rife, often worsened by the Blitz and evacuation process. Communal shelters in large cities did sometimes force middle class and working class residents to sit side by side, forging a communal spirit. Yet the frequent shortage of bomb shelters meant the wealthy were prioritised. During the Blitz many of London's wealthy residents left the city in pursuit of the safer countryside where they owned property or could pay for a temporary rural retreat. Some even moved abroad entirely. Stewart Hylton's research has revealed that 17 of the 37 houses in Hyde Park Gardens went on sale during the Blitz. In Belgrave Square, 13 of the 45 houses went on the market during the war. Thus, those with money could afford to protect themselves better than those without. Generally speaking, on the home front, wealth equalled greater protection from the bombs. In one particularly bleak case, the West End's super rich sought shelter in the basement of the Dorchester Hotel while refusing the same right to those unable to pay the door fee. Outside, a raid ensued. State provided shelters provided refuge for approximately 17.5 million people. However, an estimated 27.5 million people lived in high risk areas. The rationing system, too, was a source of inequality. Only mass produced food was rationed, meaning that those with money could afford to buy harder to source but higher quality food. Restaurants remained un-rationed allowing the well-off to dine out. Despite all of this blatant inequality and strife, the evacuation system[54] and destruction caused by bombings forced many middle and upper class citizens to take note of Britain's prevalent and widespread poverty. One traditionalist position has been to view the war as the catalyst to the

---

[54] Operation Pied Piper was organised in summer 1938, by the Anderson Committee. Provisions were made for over 4 million civilians, predominantly children, to be relocated from high risk city zones to lower risk areas. The plan was implemented on 1 September as 3.5 million people were evacuated. This was the first wave of evacuation. By March 1940, a large proportion of these evacuees had been sent home. The second wave of evacuations occurred in June 1940, after the fall of France.

post-war welfare state.[55] Yet, it is more accurate to see it as the *accelerator* for such reforms, because of its illuminating capabilities.

The post-war Labour party based much of its revolutionary welfare reforms on the findings of Liberal Minister, William Beveridge. Beveridge published his report on poverty in 1942. He examined the British population's economic position at a time when state support had never been so extensive. The wartime coalition quickly mobilised the economy. Many industries were nationalised and greater state relief was provided.[56] Two thirds of British funds went to the war effort as Keynesian economics was adopted. Keynes pushed for the government to use its budgetary and revenue powers to raise capital, which would then be reinvested into the economy thereby increasing productivity and creating an artificial economic boost. Taxation massively increased during the war. For example, purchase tax was raised by 100% during the six years of warfare. Income tax was doubled in Kingsley Wood's April 1941 Budget.[57] A

---

[55] A view accepted by historians like Bob Holman and Paul Addison. The latter argues that by 1940 Labour Ministers were declaring that a British victory would mean a restructured Britain.

[56] Under Chamberlain the Ministry of Supplies had been formed but under Churchill the Ministry of Food, Shipping, Economic Warfare and Home Security and Information was also established. An Emergency Medical Service was formed in 1939 and by 1941 under Bevin's Essential Work Orders Act full conscription was in place.

[57] S. Broadberry and P. Howlett, 'Blood, Sweat and Tears: British Mobilisation for World War II,'

further 4 million were required to pay tax. Additional sources of taxations included Excess Profits Tax and Pay as You Earn. The latter was introduced in 1943. Thus, from early on, the war proved tight on the individual's wallet. Yet such an economic position was deemed necessary if Churchill's goal of 'total war' was to be achieved. Britain was the second most mobilised warring country after the USSR. By 1944, 23% of the working population was in the armed forces, with an equal amount working in 'group 1' industries.[58] This group included heavy industries, all directly targeted towards the war machine. As Robert MacKay states, 'the Coalition government succeeded in manipulating the economy into fitness for total war.'[59] Victory started on the home front.

* * *

I still felt a little bruised from the previous voyage and in no hurry to return to work. September brought more than just the beginning of autumn; with its shorter days and crunchy brown leaves falling from the trees. It also brought a call to report to the Liverpool docks on 8th day of the month. A voyage from Liverpool could mean we were going almost anywhere. Arriving at the docks to sign on, I was surprised to find that I was the only radio officer being appointed. I had expected a run of the mill Merchant

---

http://www2.warwick.ac.uk/fac/soc/economics/staff/sbroadberry/wp/totwar3.pdf
[58] Ibid, p.26
[59] R. MacKay, 'The Test of War: Inside Britain 1939-1945,' (London, 1999) p.80

steam ship, which huffed and puffed its way through water. However, what stood before me on that pretty autumn morning was a beautiful, luxury liner of an enormous size. I was handed paperwork as I left the dock's administrative office. It indicated that the liner was on 'Government Service'. This meant nothing to me and was why the title was chosen. The Ministry of Information had mastered the art of answering all questions by telling you nothing. Clambering aboard, I needed quite a bit of help to find out where I had to go. There was no obvious route to the Radio Room. When I eventually stumbled upon it, I found two senior radio officers who were members of the original peacetime crew.

There was a great mystery as to the nature of our next voyage. I went for a quick walk round the deck and noticed that a lot of activity was ensuing around the lifeboats. At first I thought they were merely checking that the davits[60] were in good condition, but after a while I realised that the lifeboats were being removed permanently. The prospect of not having any lifeboats was an unsettling one. Rumours were rife about what the voyage would entail. The crew had no solid information to base their theories on – it was all sheer speculation. Soon we realised what was about to occur: the davits were being adapted to support landing craft; and army supplies were being brought on board. We would be landing troops.

Shortly afterwards the troops themselves arrived. They were American and the news soon filtered back

---

[60] Mechanical devices used to lower lifeboats

that these US soldiers were fresh from their training camps. They had yet to engage in any warfare. The Reina was to join a convoy departing from the port at Liverpool on 13th September. This was unusual because ships of this size and speed usually sailed alone. But we were headed for the Mediterranean and it had acquired a grim reputation. The waters were saturated with U-Boats. Above, the Luftwaffe and Italian Air Force were a serious threat to allied ships.[61] Moreover, the remainder of the French Navy was based at Oran and was openly hostile.[62] This explained why we were in convoy and why we had a remarkably heavy defence escort surrounding us. The Reina had a rather massive armament, the most impressive being the Oerlikon guns which could be used against targets in the air and on water.[63] The installation of the landing craft was a long and laborious task, and we departed from Liverpool five days after boarding. We were with the Malta convoy and put on standby. The two senior radio officers were

---

[61] In August 1942 13 Allied ships were sunk in the Mediterranean, a loss of 110,000 tons and in September 1942 4 Allied ships sunk in the Med, a loss of 800 tons (weights approximate). No losses in this region in October 1942.

[62] On July 3rd 1940 Operation Catapult was put into place. It was the result of Churchill taking the difficult decision to open fire on the majority of the French fleet based at Oran. This resulted in the death of 1299 French seamen and wounded 350 more, but maintained the British Navy's place as the largest naval force in Europe. It proved to the US that Britain was prepared to keep fighting.

[63] Oerlikon Contraves produced various models of 20mm cannons used during the war, predominantly by the Allies, on ships as anti-aircraft guns.

to handle the radio traffic. My role was to keep the public address system in operation whilst maintaining the radio equipment on the ship's motor launch. The public address system was used to provide radio entertainment as well as information. Its maintenance should not have been any problem. The entertainment was provided by the BBC who broadcasted endless tracks of a funereal character, which was a real turn off for us all. Often, seaman would smash the speakers instead of simply turning them off when the broadcast proved to be dim. I did not have the facilities to keep repairing or replacing the speakers. Eventually I had to approach a relatively senior officer about the matter. I warned him that he would not be able to use the system to give out his orders if such vandalism continued. I simply could not keep pace with the damage. At this point I, like most of the crew, knew nothing about when the anticipated action would take place (or even where it would occur). I tried to strike a deal with the officer – get him to tell me when we would be making our landing and have the equipment repaired by then, but the best I could weasel out of him was that 'they' would see what they could do.

My daily routine on the Reina was fairly tedious and heavily regulated, more so than previous voyages. I awoke every morning to breakfast followed by my first tour of the decks. I had to make my rounds of all the radio equipment and duly maintain it. I had to constantly check the wires for the radios, loudspeakers and public address system. There were set times for meals, with mine being different from the two senior radio officers who were required to be on Bridge

Watch. Despite the stringent nature of everyday life on the Reina, I found myself with more leisure time than previous voyages. That was welcomed. We arrived at the port in Oran on 8th November. We very suddenly broke off from the Malta convoy and diverted towards North Africa. It was at that point that most of us knew that the troops would soon be landing. This prompted the ship's Chaplain to approach me and ask me to arrange an altar on the Bridge Deck. He planned to hold Mass before the landing. My previous experience of serving at Mass in Edinburgh did nothing to assist me here. There was no altar, no altar cloth, tabernacle, chalice, not even hymn books. My solution to the lack of an altar was an upturned tea packing case. Instead of kneelers I found a few chairs. I left the rest up to the priest who had all he needed: the wine and unleavened bread for Communion. The sacrament was provided for a substantial number of soldiers and we could see the shoreline in the distance. I remember gazing out at and imagining Vichy French troops going through the exact same protocol. The troops lining up before the priest, awaiting their spiritual nourishment to guide and protect them during the approaching battle. It was tragic that such precautions were taken by both sides, when only an hour or so later they would all prepare to kill one and other. There was great hypocrisy in this emergency Mass, and yet not having it would have been equally as disheartening because many gained great comfort and strength from it.

This was Operation Torch.[64] We landed at Arzeu Point[65] under the governance of Admiral Andrew Cunningham on 8th November 1942. The invasion was the result of the victory at the Second Battle of El Alamein in November 1942.[66] General Montgomery had finally pushed out General Rommel's Afrika Korps, regaining control of Libya and preserving Egypt. [67] This victory ended the threat of the Axis forces in North Africa and meant that the Allies now dominated the Suez Canal, a strategic naval passage through the Mediterranean. As John Keegan points out, 'the victory was down to Montgomery's skilled and conscientious planning. Montgomery's debut on the battlefield had been one of the most brilliant in the history of Generalship.'[68] The landings started at dawn and I was amazed at how quietly the engines of the landing craft sounded. During the trials, the engines had created a tremendous noise but by unknown measures the sound was subdued for the actual landings. The troops themselves were understandably subdued also. I overheard a few of them muttering to themselves that they would obey orders to get on the

---

[64] The Anglo-American invasion of North Africa, the November 1942 operation was the first time British and American troops worked together on an invasion plan.

[65] A town in North-east Oran. The Central Task Force landed at Oran and was comprised of 18,500 troops. Major-General Lloyd Fredendall commanded them.

[66] 150 miles west of Cairo, the area is desert.

[67] Nicknamed the Desert Fox, Rommel was well-respected by both sides.

[68] Sir John Keegan (1934-2012) was a highly acclaimed British military historian, author of many works regarding military history and a journalist for The Telegraph.

land but once there they would 'do their own thing and look after number one'. As the troops began to enter their landing craft and make their way towards the shore, the French opened fire at the ships. They operated a shore battery but fortunately it was twelve pounder guns and little damage occurred. They would have required an almost direct hit to cause any significant damage. There were a few holes in the side of the ship but nothing that the damage limitation crew could not handle. Once the last landing craft had been released we were ordered to back off. The Reina took off, tucked out of range from the French battery but still close enough to see the shoreline. It was here, floating in the open water with the beach a few miles away, that I had my first glimpse of MI6 operating behind enemy lines. I was making my rounds of the deck when I saw a small group of men clamber aboard from canoes. They were dressed in rough khaki garb, unshaven and unwashed. They made their way to the senior Army officers and spoke confidentially with them, not even acknowledging the rest of us. Events seemed to move quickly because, before long, we were ordered to the port of Algiers. It was there that we saw the familiar uniform of the military Red Caps. We stayed only long enough to take on a few passengers, presumably wounded, and re-joined convoy formation for the return trip. By this time the French Navy at Oran[69] had been disabled and the port

---

[69] In July 1940 Churchill took the decision to destroy most of the French Navy, based at Mers-el-Kebir. The Royal Navy opened fire on 3 July, killing 1299 French seamen and wounding a further 350. This act maintained the British Navy's status as the

captured, but the sinkings in the Mediterranean were still very heavy for Royal Navy and Merchant ships. In order to provide the escort for this exercise we had drawn escorts away from other areas. Escorts normally assisting in the North Atlantic were moved to assist in the Mediterranean. We kept the heavy escort until we arrived in British waters, and returned to Liverpool 14 days after the landing at Arzeu.

One advantage of sailing in a ship of this type was that it carried a doctor. I took advantage of this by having him examine my ankle. He recommended treatment for the injury which was classified as a 'War Accident.' I found myself referred to the Ministry of Pensions for two months treatment of rest.

---

largest in the war and made clear the British desire to keep fighting despite ultimately standing alone. Churchill later commented to Harry Hopkins (Roosevelt's personal representative) that the attack at Oran was "the turning point in our fortunes, it made the world realise that we were earnest in our intention to carry on."

Edited by Katherine Hodgson

9 – *The Sixth Voyage: The Sitting Duck*

<u>SS Clumberhall</u>: was built in 1930 for the West Hartlepool Steam Navigation Company. The Clumberhall had a gross tonnage of 5198. After the war she was renamed no fewer than four times and was broken up in Japan in June 1961.

19th March 1943: I reported to Manchester to sign on. Up until then I had been unaware that Manchester was a port for ocean bound vessels, and then I discovered the Manchester Ship Canal.[70] I arrived and soon boarded the worn out looking Clumberhall. Despite being only thirteen years old, she had the appearance and efficiency of a steam ship built prior to WWI. The engines were almost defunct and the ship moved slowly and tediously. I was promoted on this journey – elevated to Second Radio Officer. I had been the Second Radio Officer before, but only when there were just two radio officers on board. This meant my workload had been heavy. Unlike most promotions I did not receive a pay rise from the Marconi Company. However, I was no longer expected to undertake the more menial tasks which had been a prerequisite on previous voyages. The Third Radio Officer would now attend to the laborious task of cleaning the batteries and insulators.

The destination of this voyage was South America. As the Captain spoke those two magic words a vision ignited in my mind. A vibrant, exotic and colourful vision of tropical rainforests filled with wildlife and lush greenery. Of bustling street carnivals with lots of music and dancing. And long stretches of golden sand, almost too hot to touch, sitting parallel to the shimmering blue ocean where mighty sea creatures roamed. A cacophony of sound accompanied these wild images: of screeching monkeys swinging from trees in the rainforest; and the powerful and rhythmic

---

[70] Is a 36 mile long inland waterway which terminates in Manchester. It was first used in 1894.

beating of drums at a carnival where street food and talented dancers enthralled the on-lookers. This mysterious and exciting continent sent me on a vivid, dream-like journey and it was utterly hypnotic.

'*...and our final stop is Rosario, Argentina.*' The Captain's voice trickled into my ears once again. The cascading waterfalls of Argentina's temperate rainforest flashed into my mind. I longed to gaze in wonder at their beauty, and watch from afar the animals in their natural habitat. The Captain concluded the briefing and I quickly consulted my pocket map of the world. My eyes flew to the bottom of the page:

Rosario is a city in the east of Argentina, straddling the Parana River. Our ship will be sailing up the Parana River, I muttered to myself.

I scanned the map, looking for the rainforest:

The rainforest is to the west of the country, near Chile.

So I would not get to stand in awe of the waterfalls, or investigate the vast stretches of untouched forestry. With a small sigh of disappointment I put away my map and prepared for our departure. The Captain estimated our journey would take about ten days. We hoped it would not take any longer because the ship had no refrigerator, merely an icebox. The ice would last about a week and we hoped to take on fresh food within that time.

We were part of a slow convoy and were easily the slowest. It did not take long to find out that we were not able to keep up with the rest of the ships. The escorts kept falling back to check we were still afloat, but before long the Commodore decided he could no longer allow us to hold the rest back. He left us to go it alone parting with a message which became eerily familiar before the end of the voyage: 'Good bye and good luck.' We staggered on at snail's pace and were under no illusion that we were under constant watch by a small army of U-Boats. Our only explanation for our continued existence was that the enemy thought we were such an obvious target, and so blatantly helpless, that we must surely be a decoy. It would therefore be unwise of the U-Boats to give away their position by destroying us. Fortunately, the Lascar stokers on board worked tirelessly to fire the furnaces with coal. This kept us going in the right direction, albeit very slowly. We eventually arrived at the mouth of the River Plate, our passage into Uruguay.[71] The only intruders we had seen were a few South American fighter planes who 'buzzed' us. This meant they swooped down towards us to investigate the ship and show some bravado. They were no doubt hoping to explain this rather odd vessel which was flying a British flag but creeping along on its own in the South Atlantic.

Throughout the journey to Uruguay I was busy with additional duties. The workload was no lighter now I had been promoted, but it was less labour

---

[71] An estuary between Uruguay and Argentina. The only battle to ever take place in South America during the war occurred here in December 1939, resulting in an allied victory and the scuttling of the Graf Spee.

intensive. The Captain had asked me to prepare identity landing documents for each of the crew. In theory this was simple enough. I had to question each crew member for their particulars: name; age; family; finger prints and so forth. I then wrote a physical description of the men, based on their answers to standard questions about their physique. It was all running smoothly until I got to the Lascars. It was not the language barrier which created the biggest obstacle – they all spoke through their 'Head Man.'[72] No, the greatest obstacle was that the questions just did not seem compatible with the Lascars. Although an interpreter was present they were unable to tell me the name of their father or mother, or whether they were married or single. It all proved hopelessly difficult as they were not able to read or write. I could estimate their height and easily describe them physically but beyond that I was left with blank pages. Many of the Lascars had lost the tops their fingers through disease. When first presented with a Lascar who lacked a full finger I struggled to see how his fingerprints would be taken. However, it was really quite simple – he indeed had shorter fingers than the ones he was born with, but there was still a top to his fingers. His fingerprint would still cover his skin. So I took the fingerprints of every disfigured Lascar, pressing their stubs into the ink. The shape of the print may have been different had they had a full finger, but they could still be tracked and identified. This satisfied the Argentine and Uruguay authorities.

---

[72] He could be recognised as the man who led the Lascars as they walked in single file. He spoke adequate English.

The authorities in Uruguay were not as rigid as those in Argentina. We got the impression that the Uruguay government was more pro-British than the Argentines. We first headed for the engineering works at Montevideo, where they were going to try to improve our engines. This granted us a few extra days to enjoy the extraordinary hospitality of the locals. We were welcomed wherever we went and invited into the homes of the British ex-pat community, who also took us round the shops to complete our shopping lists. Although I enjoyed shopping in Uruguay I still had sad memories of all the presents which I had bought in Boston. Presents now lying at the bottom of the Atlantic. Every time I paid for an item, I fervently told myself that what I bought here would get back home safely. We then headed up river to the meat packing station, to load up with the now staple UK diet of tinned corned beef. As we approached the factory I noticed a large black cloud overhead. As the ship trundled along and we eventually rolled beneath the apparent 'cloud' I realised that it was in fact a swarm of flies. Thousands of flies were feeding off the parts of the meat which had been rejected for canning. The Clumberhall stopped, anchored neatly into the harbour at the meat packing factory. A small man, with jet black hair and olive coloured skin strolled out from the factory, smoking a cigarette and grinning at the entire crew.

'Good day.' He called and casually waved a tanned, muscular arm in our direction.

'Come inside for a tour.' He hollered, as the Captain emerged from his room and threw the man a suspicious look.

'Everybody on the ship – come down.'

The Captain hurried off the ship and onto the deck. Running up to the man, he grabbed him gently by the shoulder and said:

'We're here to collect the tinned meat. I presume you're aware of our order?'

'Of course Sir!' scoffed the man, as he exhaled a large cloud of smoke.

'But first – we tour.' And he waved in the direction of the ship, indicating that the entire crew should follow him inside.

We were given a tour of their production line. The gentleman turned out to be the factory manager. He led the crew, flanked by our Captain, around his large imposing factory. He seemed immensely proud of the tight affair he was running. His English was broken but decent enough for us to understand the general idea of what he was saying. He smoked the entire time and after explaining to everyone how a particular part of the factory worked he would turn to our Captain and make a joke under his breath, usually followed by a loud, roaring laugh from himself and a muffled chuckle from the Captain. Starting at the slaughter house, the manager led us through the factory and finished by showing us the canning and labelling process. I was puzzled to see the cans being separated into two stacks – one on the left and one on the right –

and rather intrigued as to the difference. It transpired that the only difference was the label: one label for the UK market; and the other for elsewhere.

We soon took our leave of Uruguay and headed for Buenos Aires. Again we were impressed by the welcome from the British community. They not only took us back to their home for meals, but took us shopping and for leisurely evening drives and boat trips. Chatting to the locals and expats, tales of the scuttling of the Graf Spee in 1940 were rife.[73] It was their Blitzkrieg. Leaving Argentina, we headed back home as part of a convoy. It came as no real surprise when the Clumberhall slipped behind from the rest of the convoy. Despite the engineers' efforts in Uruguay to improve her engine power, the Clumberhall barely dragged herself across the South Atlantic. As we trundled through the seemingly never-ending stretches of ocean, I was again all too conscious of the fact that we were sailing in open water and totally defenceless. The journey back felt even longer than the wearisome outward journey. We took a detour – rolling into the Straits of Gibraltar to join another convoy. I was on bridge watch as we entered the Straits and I could see the lights on the shoreline off the port bow. I was soon relieved of my duties, allowed to go below for a short four hour sleep. In due course I was awakened by a gentle nudge and call of my name. With a sleepy nod and heavy yawn, I slowly rose out of bed and took a quick sip of the cocoa being handed to me. Consumed with fatigue which made my eyes droop and limbs

---

[73] Following the battle of the River Plate on 13 December 1939, the German battleship, the Graf Spee was scuttled at Montevideo.

ache, I stumbled onto the bridge and there, to my surprise, I could see the lights on the shoreline off the port bow. It was exactly as I had seen it hours earlier. The ship did not have enough power to beat the tide in the Straits, and now we were forced to wait for the tide to turn. There was a cold wind. I stood on the bridge in the darkness, staring at the flickering harbour lights. There was a comforting sense of tranquillity – nothing but the dark night air, gentle ripple of the waves and the glow of the lights in the distance.

Approximately four to five hours later the tide turned. We made our way into the harbour at Gibraltar, through the boom. It was not very long before we got our orders for the return journey, as part of another convoy. We retraced our steps through the Straits and pointed towards Britain. It again came as no real surprise when we found that we could not keep up with the accompanying ships. The familiar goodbye message from the Commodore echoed through the Clumberhall as we paddled our lonely way up the Atlantic. Although I did not realise it at the time, I learned an important lesson on this voyage. It was triggered when I noticed my alarm clock had gone from my cabin. That evening I complained loudly at the mess table about this. I was surprised by the reaction from the Captain and other officers. The Captain said that that theft was 'not something to happen on my ship.' None of them would believe that my alarm clock had been stolen. It was a brand new alarm clock, hard to get your hands on in those days. I felt compelled to repeat my complaint the following evening. I was too naïve to realise that the Captain was creating the scenario where he could provide the remedy himself without having to record the theft in the Ship's Log. Official records of theft led to ramifications when the voyage ended. A few days later the alarm clock appeared on the floor outside my cabin and I joyfully announced this to all. Unimpressed, the Captain responded: 'Well it never really happened, did it? It wasn't stolen.' It was only then that I realised what was happening. The Captain was not addressing the issue head-on. In acting as if it had never been stolen he was applying the age old doctrine: seamen never steal from their shipmates. The only time it is necessary to lock away your valuables is when the ship is in port.

We had long been on this voyage, and the constant fear that at any moment your life could be ended was beginning to have an effect on morale. Even with the tightest discipline we were very nervy and on edge. There was constant bickering and complaints, mostly about the food. It required great determination for each of us to keep control of our feelings. This was known as 'going home' sickness. However, an impromptu detour helped to alleviate the crew's frustrations on our homeward journey. Sailing along in the middle of the Atlantic, we got a message from the Admiralty addressed to all ships in the area. Major German battleships had moved away from their attack area and were heading north towards Europe. These German ships were the Scharnhorst[74] and the

---

[74] Laid down in 1935 and commissioned in 1939, the Scharnhorst was a large German battleship. Sunk on 26th December 1943, the

Gneisenau[75] and their supporting vessels. The Admiralty warned us to get out of the way – and do so fast. We were advised to go to Ponta Delgada in the Azores[76] and stay there until we got further instructions. There was quite a scurry to find the Azores on the map and then Ponta Delgada.[77] Fortunately, the Second Mate – who was our navigator – knew the area relatively well and our hide-out spot turned out to be fairly close by. It was not long before we were admiring a very new and novel shoreline. Pulling in at Ponta Delgada, I felt like I had been transported back in time. The harbour and surrounding countryside was like something from The Lost World.[78] From the deck I gazed in surprise at a sheep cart on the dusty road before me. It was much like an ordinary cart, although fairly small in size, but a sheep was harnessed to the cart and pulling it along. This small, primitive land – marooned off in the middle of the Atlantic Ocean, hidden away from decades of industrialisation, was part of neutral Portugal. After lengthy explanations via the British

---

ship had previously been called the 'Lucky Scharnhorst' by the Germans.

[75] The Gneisenau was the other ship in the class alongside the Scharnhorst. The former was laid down in 1934 and commissioned in 1938. It was sunk on 28th March 1945.

[76] An archipelago in the Atlantic which is part of Portugal. Sao Miguel is the biggest island and it is home to Ponta Delgada.

[77] Ponta Delgada is the capital of Sao Miguel and sits on the south-east coast of the island. The municipality is also of the capital of the whole Azores.

[78] A 1912 novel by Sir Arthur Conan Doyle. Set in the South American rainforest, four men uncover prehistoric dinosaurs and creatures.

Consulate explaining why we were there, we were allowed to stay at Ponta Delgada and come ashore.

Upon arriving ashore, the HMS Chanticleer was quickly spotted.[79] She was tied up not too far from the Clumberhall and had been damaged, kept in port until she was seaworthy. We were soon joined by a shipload of Navy seamen. Although not much of a drinker in those days I had a particular fondness for gin and orange. I had a surfeit of gin but no orange juice. The Navy personnel had no gin and a surfeit of orange juice. So we got along famously. Aside from our gin soaked meals, late night conversations and card games, I took a little bit of time to explore Ponta Delgada. Despite my hazy memory, I recall colourful botanical gardens, lush foliage and vegetation and a sweet aroma which filled the air. The land was beautiful. The sea was a glorious aquamarine and the sky a bright blue. The Azores' fertile soil and warm climate meant there was plenty of fresh fruit and vegetables. I started my days with a ripe banana and fresh cup of coffee, by mid-morning everyone would tuck into the island's sweet, crunchy apples and at lunchtime crisp lettuce would accompany a fresh piece of fish along with the island's very own exotic strawberry guavas and cherimoyas. The panic from the German Navy soon passed and we were told to make our way back home. The last phase of the journey back to Britain passed without trouble. The entire crew of the Clumberhall was very conscious of

---

[79] HMS Chanticleer was a Black Swan Class sloop damaged by a torpedo from U-515 east of the Azores. She was towed to the Azores, where she was declared a total loss.

the novelty of going home after almost a year at sea. On board we had no laundry service and dirty clothes had become a big problem. To clean our clothes we filled a bucket with hot water and took a bar of soap to them. If we could not dry the clothing on a line then the engineers (if in a tolerant mood) would let us use the engine room. However, leaving clothes to dry in a room kept warm by a coal engine gave our clothes a very grubby appearance as soot coated the fabric. On 6th February 1944 I bade farewell to the Clumberhall for the last time. I signed off at West Hartlepool. I was not sorry to see the back of that particular voyage or vessel.

10 – The Naval Turning Point: Farewell to the 'Happy Time'

Spring 1943 was a crucial turning point in the Battle of the Atlantic. For the first time in the Battle's entirety, German vessels were being lost at a higher rate than Allied ones. The British, Commonwealth and US navies now dominated the North Atlantic.

Until then, the Battle of Atlantic proved to be a problematic factor for the British military. An average of 920 tons was lost daily in 1941/2. A huge volt-face occurred and in April and May 1943 a total of 55 U Boats were destroyed.[80] By 23rd May 1943 Doenitz called off the full scale offensive in the Atlantic. It would not be surprising if the death of his younger son, Peter, on 19th May (killed in the North Atlantic) contributed to Doenitz's decision. However, the sudden rate at which submarines were being lost was also an attribute. After 23rd May, U-Boats did remain in the Atlantic. They were a constant lurking threat, but the sheer quantity of submarines, and their sinister and insidious presence, diminished greatly. So what was it about that relatively short period which so dramatically changed the fortunes of the Allied

---

[80] 15 in April, 40 in May.

Navies? As B.B. Schofield[81] notes, 'the fact that it happened so suddenly caused much heart-searching in the U-Boat command.'[82]

Prior to the summer of 1940 U-Boat access to the North Atlantic had been restricted. The Kriegsmarine lacked a heavy U-Boat presence in regions where the British Navy was most vulnerable. As such, the Kriegsmarine resorted to dropping minefields in the straits of Dover as a form of offensive attack. Coastal Command was in charge of reconnaissance for the Channel. The Royal Navy patrolled the North Sea and Iceland-Faroe Island Gap. In 1939, as First Lord of the Admiralty, Churchill introduced an offensive system were escort destroyers hunted out U-Boats and tried to sink them. This was widely used in the first year of war but to little effect. On 17th September 1939, the carrier Courageous was sunk by the U-29 in the Bristol Channel and 518 lives were lost. In the initial stages of war, escort vessels roamed the seas surrounding Britain on the prowl for U-Boats. In doing so they were inadvertently directed away from convoys. Merchant ships were therefore left highly vulnerable to attacks, and unsurprisingly were

---

[81] Vice Admiral B.B. Schofield had a distinguished and long career in the Navy. He served in both World Wars and was part of the team planning the D Day Landings. He has written books on both the British Air Force and Navy during both wars.

[82] Schofield, B.B. 'The Defeat of the U-Boats during World War II,' Journal of Contemporary History, Vol. 16, (1988), The Second World War: Part 1, p.128

frequently torpedoed as a result. In 1940 alone the British lost 471 ships (2,186,158 tons).[83]

Such losses would only increase as U-Boats became more active in the Atlantic. It was the fall of France in June 1940 which granted the Kriegsmarine the opportunity to become a truly great threat. Prior to that, the U-Boats had yet to make their mark. Despite high allied loss rates in 1940, the Kriegsmarine also suffered many causalities. In the early months of war 23 U-boats were destroyed. Entering the war with only 57 submarines, 46 of which were operational, Doenitz had lost almost half of his catalogue in less than a year.[84] But all of this was turned upside down once German expansion across Western European intensified. Doenitz's submarines quickly established themselves as a powerhouse of offence; capable of sinking tens of thousands of tons of allied cargo and battle ships. Occupying France meant U-Boat pens were established along the French coast, at locations such as Lorient, St Nazaire and La Rochelle. Thus, the Kriegsmarine gained direct access to the North Atlantic and the Merchant vessels roaming it. Occupying France had given the U-boat campaign the chance to strengthen and improve, it was the starting trigger for a long string of German victories at sea. But it was Doenitz's tactics which were the *catalyst* to the Kriegsmarine's so called 'happy time.'

German submariners experienced two 'happy times.' The first wave was from summer 1940 to,

---

[83] Ibid, p.123
[84] Ibid, p.120

roughly, early 1941. This 'wave' marks the first significant stretch of time when the Kriegsmarine was sinking huge numbers of Merchant vessels and their cargo, and experiencing little loss themselves. In the thirteen months after the fall of France, 606 Allied ships were sank (3,206,096 tons). Historians dispute the exact date in which the first wave came to a close. One popular answer is March 1941, when the Kriegsmarine lost three of its most valued U-Boat commanders. Renowned and popular ace, Gunther Prien, went missing along with his 45 man crew on 7th March 1941. Prien spent less than 2 years at sea commanding the U-47. Under Prien's command the U-47 sank 30 vessels. In October 1940 Prien formed his own Wolfpack, named 'Group Prien.' The group sank 32 vessels, amounting to 175,000 tons of cargo. Prien was the first ace to receive the Knight's Cross of the Iron Cross.[85] He received the exalted Knight's Cross with Oak Leaves in October 1940. This was the highest award within the German military. Joachim Schepke was also a recipient of the prestigious Oak Leaves medal. The notable commander was killed in action on 17th March 1941. He had commanded the U-100 for 5 patrols before it was damaged by depth charges from HMS Walker and HMS Vanoc. Forced to surface, the U-100 was then rammed by Vanoc and 38 men were killed – including Schepke. The U-100 was a highly successful submarine, responsible for the loss of 137,819 tons of allied cargo. The final ace lost

---

[85] Ritterkreuz des Eisernen Kreuzes in German, the now obsolete award was given to holders of the Knight's Cross for exceptional bravery on the battlefield.

in March 1941 was Otto Kretschmer. A highly revered seaman, he is widely considered the most successful U-Boat commander of the Second World War. Kretschmer was responsible for the sinking of 47 ships and 274,333 tons. He was taken prisoner by the British in March 1941, spending the rest of the war in British and Canadian POW camps. He died in 1998. Occurring during the first 'happy time' was the full implementation of Doenitz's 'Wolfpacks'. This system involved stray U-Boats, reconnaissance aircraft and radio intelligence locating a convoy.[86] U-Boats positioned near the convoy would then receive instructions from the headquarters in Lorient to form a pack and approach said convoy, often by surrounding it. It remained a highly effective system for some time. In 1942, for example, 86 U-Boats were lost compared to 1,160 British ships. As Schofield retrospectively noted, this was 'a loss rate that could not be sustained indefinitely.'[87]

Doenitz replaced Admiral Raeder as Commander of the Kriegsmarine in January 1943. However, the skill and efficiency he had displayed in leading the U-Boats could not be continued at a larger scale. As the allies' technology, tactics and manufacturing improved German supremacy in the North Atlantic diminished rapidly. Qualitative improvements took gradual effect and contributed to an Allied victory in

---

[86] Increased bases in Norway and France allowed the Germans to increase their use of long range aircraft. The Focke-Wulf FW200 'Kondor' aircraft was frequently used for patrols over the Atlantic.
[87] Ibid

the campaign. No one factor alone explains the sudden change of fortunes for the Allies. So what were the specific changes that led to this water borne triumph? What changes had been implemented but only truly came into full effect in the spring of '43?

One important factor was breaking the Enigma Code. Ironically this breakthrough was the result of a German invention twenty years earlier. In 1923 Dr Arthur Scherbius developed a machine similar to a typewriter, able to transcribe coded information. Scherbius targeted his invention at private companies. His machine scrambled letters in a coded message. As long as the decoder understood exactly how to set the rotor on the machine, he or she could decode the message by accurately repositioning the letters. In the same year Scherbius established the Chiffriermaschinen Aktiengesellschaft – the Cipher Machines Corporation – in Berlin. Three years later, the German Navy developed their own version of the product for sea bound communications. Various editions of the machine existed throughout the German military by 1933. But in 1931 a German spy granted the French permission to photograph a stolen Enigma manual. Unable to interpret the manual, the French handed their information over to the Poles. The Polish Cipher Bureau quickly made tracks in deciphering the manual. Within a couple of years the Polish Cipher Bureau had built its very own Enigma machine. From 1933 to 1939 the Bureau was reading the Wehrmacht's internal messages. In 1939, the Polish Cipher Bureau passed their knowledge onto the British government. This was retained at Bletchley

Park, located in a secluded part of Buckinghamshire. With coded messages being used by all parts of the German military, mathematicians and problem solvers at Bletchley were kept busy. Despite this, the site and its business was kept top secret; and was codenamed Station X.

For the staff at Bletchley, a key aim was breaking the codes used by the Kriegsmarine in the North Atlantic. If the Allies knew in advance where U-Boats were positioned they could redirect ships out of dangerous territory. In early 1941 a German trawler was captured near Norway. Found on board were two Enigma machines and a list of Enigma settings used by the Kriegsmarine. It was the perfect find. The Allies had their hands on the very codes used by the enemy. Within a month of the find, in April 1941, Station X was able to read fluently Enigma messages. In May 1941 another capture led to further German code books. This time the books contained the codes for future months. The German weather ship, Munchen, was attacked and found on board were the codes for June 1941. In June 1941 two more German ships were captured, containing the codes for July. Bletchley Park staff could now decode messages to coincide with upcoming events, giving the allied navies a new degree of foresight. Unsurprisingly, three U-Boats were ambushed in the Mediterranean in September 1941.

Significant changes to the convoy system must also be considered when evaluating what caused allied supremacy in the North Atlantic. In 1942 Professor Patrick Blackett was appointed Director of

Operational Research for the Admiralty. This position was held until 1945. In '42 Blackett, and a team of researchers, studied the efficiency of convoys. Presenting the admiralty with some unexpected results, Blackett revealed that convoys were more efficient as larger bodies. Typically, only one ship in a convoy would sink when attacked. Thus, the lager the convoy – the smaller the overall loss. Furthermore, larger convoys allowed for fewer trips across the Atlantic, thereby reducing the *potential* for loss.

Increasing the size of convoys was only possible if ships could be produced and repaired at a sufficient speed. A major problem facing the British Navy was its inability to produce ships at an adequate pace. All of that was about to change with the help of the Americans. US support empowered the Allied Navies, allowing them to gain access to more ships and to build ones at a high, efficient rate. One particular advantage was the addition of 50 vintage WWI American destroyers given to the British and Canadian Navies. On 2nd September 1940 the USA lent the destroyers, in return receiving the use of naval and air bases in British colonies. The Americans now had access to bases in locations such as Newfoundland and the Caribbean.[88] Other support came from the unofficial ally in 1941. From as early as May of that year, US ships began to escort Merchant vessels. But the greatest contribution of all was the signing of the Lend Lease Act on 11th March 1941. Stated in the Act was the President's right to 'sell, transfer title to,

---

[88] Formally known as the 'Destroyers for Bases' Agreement, the deal was FDR's alternative to cash transactions.

exchange, lease, lend, or otherwise dispose of, to any such government [whose defence the President deems vital to the defence of the United States] any defence article.' Important resources were, therefore, increasingly being ferried across the North Atlantic from the USA. Following the enactment of Lend Lease half of all food entering Britain came from the United States. From 1941 two thirds of other resources travelled from America to reach Britain. Although vital to British military survival, Lend Lease caused growing numbers of Merchant vessels to make the dangerous journey across the Atlantic. And with them, increasingly valuable cargo. This integral piece of policy proved to be a bit of a double edged sword. It forced Merchant vessels to carry growing numbers of important goods across the Atlantic, making these ships more important – and more vulnerable. As a result of this and improved U-Boat tactics and bases, the Allied Navies were losing larger quantities of cargo. In the first six months of 1942, 526 ships were sunk. The total for the entire year was an astounding 1,160 ships (6,266,215 tons).[89] The U-Boats threatened to literally starve Britain into defeat.

Officially entering the war on the Allied side in December 1941, the Americans presented another asset of great importance. Not only could they offer goods, money and further manpower but could bring to an end the cripplingly slow production rates of the Allied Navies. The US, skilled at mass production, was able to build vessels at a faster rate than the

---

[89] Schofield, p.124

British and Commonwealth forces. Pre-fabricated vessels, like the Liberty, were rapidly produced and used to replace ships damaged and destroyed by U-Boat attacks. The Liberty was a class of ship. Based on a British naval concept, it was adapted by the Americans and solely built in the United States. Praised for its low cost efficient design, the Liberty was heavily relied upon. Liberty ships were used by the US Navy, and the British and Soviets under the Lend Lease Agreement. Eighteen American shipyards set to work producing the Liberty class. Around 2,710 Liberty ships were built between 1941 and 1945, with 3 ships finished a day by early 1943. This contrasts starkly with Doenitz's meagre 250 submarines commissioned in 1942, as the Kriegsmarine's commander underestimated the number of losses he would experience the following year. By early 1943 the Allies were able to maintain high numbers of vessels despite substantial U-Boat attacks. They had finally out-produced Doenitz; even though the problem of the torpedo and the deadly Wolfpacks from which they were often fired could never be eradicated completely.

Increasing convoy sizes did not *solely* equate to more vessels. It also meant using overheard aircraft for greater coverage. In 1990 Canadian historian Marc Milner wrote that air coverage in the Atlantic was 'a subject [that] mainstream air enthusiasts ignore utterly and naval historians treat only in passing.'[90] As Milner duly points out, it was a feature which proved to be

---

[90] J. Gooch (ed.) 'Decisive Campaigns of the Second World War,' (London, 1990), p. 59.

highly effective in the Allied fight for the Atlantic. With overhead support, U-Boats feared surfacing; planes could easily spot them and fire directly at them. Furthermore, planes could attack the Kondor – the Kriegsmarine's overhead escort. Yet gathering enough air cover took some time. Professor Blackett's suggestions had included increasing overhead protection, but this was met with a degree of opposition. At the same time as Blackett was calling for more air coverage in the Atlantic, Bomber Command were demanding more to facilitate their extensive campaign. Initially Churchill had sided with the Air Force. But at sea, new planes had to be developed so the infamous Mid Atlantic Gap could be closed. The Gap stretched approximately 600 miles south from Cape Farewell to the Azores. Within this area air coverage was practically non-existent. Prior to 1943 long range aircraft had yet to be developed adequately. Planes could go so far before they had to turn back and refuel. Attempts had, of course, been made to try and overcome this. Early in the war, the fighter aircraft the Hurricane was being taken to the mid-Atlantic, and catapulted from the decks of specially adapted ships. These were called Catapult Aircraft Merchant ships, or CAMs. But this was hardly practicable. The Hurricane could fire one shot and then had to be ditched in the sea. In October 1942 Sir Amos Ayre, Director of Merchant Shipbuilding, commissioned twelve ships to be adapted for the purpose of launching planes from their decks. Six tankers and six bulk grain ships were fitted with long, flat decks – perfect for fighter planes to take off.[91] These twelve ships were named the 'Mac ships.' The Mac ships have received relatively little recognition; often overlooked because of the integral role played by the B-24D Liberator. The Liberator was a long-range aircraft able to travel across the Gap. It had been commissioned in 1941 but until late 1942 was out of Coastal Command's hands, away from the Atlantic and used by Bomber Command instead. One important point to make is that the emphasis placed on intensive bombing meant sea defence was neglected. As such, the struggle in the Atlantic arguably dragged on for much longer than necessary. Unsurprisingly, Bomber Harris's decision to bomb U-Boat pens has been a widely criticised one. And it was a decision which would be later revoked, instead concentrating greater resources into Coastal Command.

Advancements in weaponry also proved useful to the allied navies by early 1943. Depth charges had long been a staple part of Atlantic warfare, having been reintroduced following the Great War. By 1943

---

[91] The Fairey Swordfish was a Royal Navy aircraft, evolved from the prototype Fairey TSR.III (Torpedo Spotter Reconnaissance). The Swordfish first flew in 1934 and entered service in 1936. A total of 2391 Swordfish aircraft was built. The Fairey Swordfish was deemed obsolete by the outbreak of war but remained in active service throughout the war, even outliving its intended replacement The Albacore. The **Fairey Swordfish Mk.II** was built in 1943. The **Mk.II LS326** became part of the 'L' Flight of 836 Squadron. This model was on board the MAC ship Rapana, on North Atlantic Convoy duties.
http://www.fleetairarmoa.org/news/swordfish-flies-for-documentary-film-on-battle-of-the-atlantic

anti-submarine weaponry had substantially improved. Depth charges were small bombs dropped into the water close to a submarine, intended to destroy or severely damage the target. The submarine was thus exposed to a hydraulic shock. In 1939 the Royal Navy designated the Mark VII. This bomb had the capacity to fall to depths of 250ft. The following year seamen attached cast iron weights to the bomb forcing it to fall deeper. The Mark VII had an amatol charge of 290lb (130kg) and was able to split a submarine pressure hull from a distance of 20ft. In 1943 the United States commissioned Mark 9. The new and improved depth charge weighed 200lb (91kg) and could sink to 600ft. It was lighter, faster and more efficient. As depth charges improved in 1943 so did allied fortunes. In 'Black May' Doenitz's U-Boats had lost one quarter of their strength; in a single month losses became unsustainable.[92] But the role of the depth charge should not be overstated. It was an effective weapon but was used *collectively,* as part of a well-oiled machine: that of the convoy, the intelligence and the weaponry. Most U-boats sunk by depth charges were not destroyed by a single charge. Several charges had to be fired, leading to an eventual collapse. This accumulation could potentially take hours.

Intelligence advancements did not just stop with the cracking of Enigma. In fact, other inventions led to better reconnaissance *on water and in flight.* This was, arguably, more effective than the improvements made to sea-bound bombs. One overwhelmingly important

---

[92] http://www.history.co.uk/study-topics/history-of-ww2/battle-of-the-atlantic

invention was that of the Cavity Magnetron. Now responsible for the microwave, in 1940 John Randall and Harry Boot stumbled upon this intelligent mechanism in Birmingham. Randall and Boot had created something totally revolutionary. It was something which revolutionised more than just the culinary world, but also dramatically improved military radar. Prior to the Cavity Magnetron, radar systems had a wavelength of one and a half metres. Radar technology had been large and awkward. But the Cavity Magnetron was a valve that split pulses of microwave radio energy, doing so on a wavelength of 10cm. Small, compact radar could now fit inside planes. This invention also led to improved ASDIC. Naval radar was now operating at a higher frequency and as such became more accurate. The prototype was handed over to the Americans in autumn 1940. In return FDR agreed to mass produce the item; free of charge. By November 1940 the Cavity Magnetron was being mass produced and it was installed in American and British planes in 1941.

Further radar improvements came in the form of High Frequency Direction Finding (H/F or Huff Duff to sailors). Huff Duff was a high powered radio direction finder. The technology itself was hardly new. In fact, radar systems were first invented in 1904. By the mid-1930s Robert Watson-Watt had developed the foundations for Huff Duff as superintendent of the Bawdsey Research Station.[93] By 1942 a radio

---

[93] Watson-Watt was a distant relative of the famous engineer, James Watt. In 1935 Watson-Watt successfully bounced radar (with a wavelength of 50m) from a transmitter to a bomber.

direction finder was developed and being fitted on British ships. The equipment was able to provide bearings of high frequency radio transmitters used by U-Boats. Including a large, rather obtrusive antenna, the Allies could intercept U-boat messages and track down the exact position of the vessel. It has been estimated that approximately 24% of U-Boats sunk, were done so because of H/F. However, it was not enough for one ship to know at any given point where the nearby submarines where. A holistic approach to intelligence had to be taken. And so it was.

In the opening months of 1943 the weather was 'exceptionally severe and hampered both the attacker and attacked.'[94] Despite these natural set-backs, intelligence allowed the allied navies to gain an upper hand. Knowing the location of submarines and where they intended to go was a good defensive method; ships could thus avoid danger zones. Cargo and lives were more likely to be saved. However, the allied navies had also improved their weaponry and this was another factor which would help to protect prized Merchant vessels. The increasing efficiency of convoys and their escorts was of course a further defensive and proactive way to ensure allied losses were reduced. As aforementioned, many (if not all) of these changes required the support of America and its money. But as vital as American support was it took

---

The famed Dowding System of the Battle of Britain owes its inception to Watson-Watt. After 1936 Watson-Watt and his team at the Bawdsey Research Station developed radar towers and were able to track aircraft.
[94] Schofield, p.126

almost two years after their entry into war for Doenitz to finally be the underdog in the Atlantic. Therefore, it was qualitative (collective) improvements which led to Allied supremacy in the Atlantic. A combination of factors worked together: improved weaponry, intelligence and methods. And these factors climaxed in spring 1943.

11 – The Seventh Voyage: D Day and Beyond

<u>The SS Evagoras</u>: a 5197 (gross) tonnage steamship, completed in 1929 in Port Glasgow. Originally called the Darsheil she was renamed the Evagoras in 1932. The Evagoras was broken up in 1954.

March 4, 1944. After spending just under a month in Edinburgh I received orders to travel south to Newcastle, where I would be joining the SS Evagoras. As the name implies, this ship was formerly part of the Greek Merchant Navy. Its arrival in the British Merchant Navy was purely to fill the blank spaces on the Admiralty's list. The SS Evagoras was the standard size for a 'tramp'[95] – approximately 5190 tons. As the Evagoras was being handled by Douglas and Ramsay Shipping Agents of Glasgow, I automatically assumed we would be travelling to North America. I would soon find out that I was right.

On my initial voyages I had kept a diary. I had documented all my experiences: the ones I relished; learned from; and endured. I also noted the sights I saw, and the people I encountered. It was a surprisingly therapeutic habit to have whilst in the midst of warfare. My diary had been lost when I was torpedoed in 1942 and I had failed to pick up my pen and start writing again. Perhaps I was simply jaded from losing so many material items when the Cape Race sank. By losing my diary I not only lost a physical thing, but a profoundly sentimental object. I found it difficult to recreate what I had already written. Writing about the day you've just had, when the events and emotions are still fresh in your mind is much easier than writing about what happened to you months, or even years, earlier. On my return to Edinburgh in February 1944, I had purchased several new notepads in the hope that I would start writing

---

[95] A name for a typical Merchant cargo ship

again. I would also use the notepads to keep track of tasks I had to do. That way, I would always be organised on board.

I returned home after buying several new notepads. I sat down at my desk and picked up my pen. A fresh, lined page lay before me. I scribbled down the date in the margin, at the top left hand corner: 15/02/44. 'Wartime Diary': Volume 2' was the heading. I quickly sketched out a to-do list for the next week, listing all the items I had to buy before my next voyage:

...Lighter petrol ...shaving soap ...toothpaste ...toilet soap ...postage stamps ... several books and papers to read

* * *

Settling into my cabin on the SS Evagoras I checked that my bag was packed with everything on my list. It was. We set sail – I had all the necessary items to aid me on the journey and the motivation to start writing again. I truly believed I would manage to keep my diary religiously. I felt confident about both my upcoming voyage and my writing.

The SS Evagoras sailed round the Pentland Firth. It stopped at Tobermory Bay on the Isle of Mull and joined a North Atlantic convoy. The convoy continued south to Liverpool where it assembled with further ships and departed. We were all immediately impressed with the improved routine and efficiency of the convoy system. No longer were we being escorted by a few fishing boats loaded with guns, but rather numerous naval warships and overhead planes.[96] It was very comforting. The convoy itself contained some Merchant vessels carrying aircraft which were catapulted over the bow, increasing our aerial protection. These light escort carriers had been used since September 1941 and were deemed a positive addition to the fight against the U-Boats. The convoy also contained some newer merchantmen converted to an aircraft carrier by having a flight deck built on them. [97] There was no shortage of action during the voyage, we had a succession of attacks both night and day but the new rockets we used all turned the dark into daylight, while the old type of depth charges were now replaced by scatter projectors which spread the explosives over a greater area. The increased convoy escorts put up a very impressive barrage while the Commodore had us all twisting and turning to confuse the U-Boats, and had everyone on board hoping that it did not also confuse the navigators.

We had a brief spell in the Mid-Atlantic when our escorts were sparse. The aircraft overhead and smaller support vessels had to return to base or face running out of fuel. This period was brief and it was not long before we saw the greatly appreciated units of the Canadian Navy and Canadian aircraft.

It was bitterly cold throughout the journey. A thick winter chill hung in the air across the Mid Atlantic. Apart from following a fixed timetable for receiving wireless messages, I spent most of my time on bridge

---

[96] Such as the Short Sunderland Flying Boats
[97] A commercial Merchant ship

watch and this was mostly on signalling duties with both flags and the Aldis Lamp for visual signalling. The brutally cold weather meant there was no danger of myself, or any of my colleagues, falling asleep while on watch. On this voyage, we could see some of the escorts from the deck, all or most of the time. This differed from previous voyages when escort vessels were always a long way away. The convoy took the usual route via Nova Scotia and headed south to New York. That would be our final destination and we arrived at the Big Apple on April 21st 1944. New York had not changed much since my last visit. Everything looked new and expensive, a booming materialistic city – the home of Western capitalism. Roaming around that shiny, roaring metropolis was exciting. The novelty did not wear off quickly. During our few, short days in New York I went shopping and toured the city, venturing to some of its most iconic sites. A warm afternoon allowed a few friends and me to take the ferry to Liberty Island and ascend Lady Liberty herself. The view from the top was breathtaking. One evening, on the way to a pub for some drinks, we gazed in awe at the mighty Empire State building. It loomed over Manhattan and its pretty lights illuminated the sky above. Each morning I would wander the busy streets of Manhattan. Rush hour had a buzz which infected the island's long, grey pavements and tall, grey buildings. The streets were crammed with bodies, chatter and ambition – the suits craving their next big promotion; the Wall Street bankers and stock brokers desperately hoping for a successful day. The taxis screeching to a halt in front of stop lights, their bright yellow paint work bringing a brief touch of light and colour to the modern concrete jungle I temporarily inhabited. The aroma of freshly brewed coffee wafted through the streets as workers, mothers, wives and children all tucked into breakfast in the apartments above. The side alleys were grimy, dark, smoke filled sites to behold; as drunks stumbled through them, the stench of alcohol still strong – and their mind and body still stuck in the previous evening's escapades.

The outward journey involved passing through the ship canal at Maine, and the same course was taken on the way back. It was an orderly and efficient route. As on the way out, we encountered many attacks from lurking U-Boats but these were quickly and robustly being countered by our numerous escorts. Apart from a brief spell of loneliness in the Mid-Atlantic we could see aircraft coming over from Iceland to usher us into British waters. The inward journey had one significant difference to the one outwards: we were travelling up the English Channel to dock in London, rather than returning to Liverpool. This was so we could unload the cargo in London. We must have arrived in London in late May or early June, however I cannot trace nor remember the exact date. The journey back had deliberately been a slow and laborious one – in preparation of the D Day Landings (at that time, something of a mystery to all on board). Approaching the docks in London I was instantly hit by the chaotic nature of the place. The South East continued to be pounded by aircraft, flying bombs and the shore batteries from France. As a result, London docklands were bedlam. When the Evagoras finally got inside the docks, she had been well and truly plastered by bombs. Luckily the damage was relatively minimal and no one on board was seriously injured or killed. The land around the Evagoras endured the most damage. I was granted a couple of day's relief while the Evagoras was unloaded and repairs were made. I went and stayed with some friends in Potters Bar.[98] It was a joy to spend two nights in a warm, comfortable bed and have a relaxing, hot bath. After my few, precious days off I returned to the docks where I boarded the Evagoras once again. She remained anchored and the crew lived on board for some time.

On June 6th 1944 Allied troops from the British, American and Canadian armies stormed the beaches at Normandy. Codenamed Operation Overlord, the long anticipated landings were the largest amphibious invasion in history with 130,000 allied troops landing on D Day alone. In doing so, they opened a second front in Western Europe.

The start of the British summer had seen Portsmouth docks filled with vessels of every size, power and appearance. It was slowly becoming obvious that D Day was imminent but just how imminent, and just where it would be taking place, remained top secret. Secrecy was the most crucial factor surrounding the approaching invasion. To maintain it, the Allies concocted Operation Fortitude. The operation involved using 'turned' German agents – who had been captured in early 1944 – to double

---

[98] Potters Bar is a town in Hertfordshire, England. It is approximately 18 miles north of Charing Cross.

cross the Germans and report back incorrect information regarding the invasion. Fortitude North involved creating false naval formations in Scotland to confuse the German intelligence. Fortitude South comprised of wide-scale naval formations across the south-coast, with fake tanks and aircraft also being built. The great deception successfully convinced the Germans that D Day would most probably occur in mid-July, in the Pas-de-Calais region somewhere between the Boulogne and Somme Estuary. On overtime since 22nd May, the teams at Bletchley Park intercepted messages at the beginning of June which confirmed Fortitude's success as the Germans prepared anti-invasion exercises between Ostend and Boulogne. Officials at Bletchley Park reported on 2nd June: 'latest evidence suggests enemy appreciates all Allied preparations completed. Expects initial landing Normandy or Brittany followed by main effort in Pas-de-Calais.'

Despite the heat wave which passed through southern England in late May and early June,[99] Eisenhower still obsessively consulted his meteorological team in the final days before the landings. The Supreme Headquarters of the Allied Expeditionary Force had originally intended the landings to take place on 5th June. However, last minute weather predictions from Eisenhower's team changed that. Led by Dr James Stagg, the meteorological team operated from Eisenhower's headquarters at Southwick House in Hampshire. On

---

[99] On 29 May temperatures of 100° Fahrenheit were recorded

The Memoirs of Alfred Hodgson

Thursday 1st June, visibility over the seas surrounding Scotland was minimal and clouds hung low. The English Channel was also turning choppy. On the evening of 2nd June, Stagg reported that the forecast for the provisional date looked unsatisfactory. 'The whole situation from the British Isles to Newfoundland has been transformed in recent days and is now full of menace.'[100] The following morning Stagg entered a further meeting with Eisenhower, armed with fresh evidence from an Irish meteorological station that Monday would not be a climatically appropriate day for an invasion. Stagg's bleak forecast for 5th forced Eisenhower to postpone the invasion, but only by 24 hours.

At 11pm on 5th June over 1200 aircraft, as part of three airborne divisions, flew towards France in preparation for the troops landing the following morning. Troops landed at five different points along the Normandy coast in the early morning of 6th June. The First US Army landed at Utah and Omaha Beaches. The US VIII Corps invaded at Utah, assisted by airborne divisions in six different zones. Within 24 hours, the US infantry held most of their planned land surrounding the Utah beach. The US V Corps landed at Omaha Beach, working a much smaller area than the troops further west. They managed to hold only a fraction of their proposed land within the first 24 hours. The British Second Army, accompanied by Canadian infantry, invaded at Gold, Juno and Sword Beaches. Facing multiple German gun batteries and

---

[100] A. Beevor, 'D-Day: The Battle for Normandy', (Penguin, 2010) p.11

Panzer counter-attacks, the Second British Army hoped to reach Caen by D Day +1.[101] Despite this objective not being achieved, some substantial ground had been made and the Allies held land as far south as Camilly, approximately 14km north of Caen. The first D Day landings had been successfully completed from landing barges and floating pontoons. To continue pushing forward with the invasion, further equipment and port facilities were required (for landing heavy equipment, supplies and troops). The Allies had anticipated the need for more docks, so had built artificial ones. Made from concrete, they were mostly on the south coast of England. The artificial docks had been tried and tested at Garlieston, on the Solway Coast. The beaches there were very similar to France's Arromanches – flat and sandy. [102] The concrete blocks, known as Mulberry Harbours, were flooded with seawater to sink them, resting on the river bed until they were required. There were two artificial harbours, towed across the English Channel and assembled just off the Normandy coastline. Mulberry A was formed by Omaha Beach and Mulberry B at Arromanches, at Gold Beach. Both harbours were six miles long, composed of flexible steel and able to hold up to 7000 tons per day. By June 18th both Mulberry A and Mulberry B were fully operational. Yet disaster struck a mere day later when a storm erupted. By June 22nd Mulberry A had been virtually destroyed and would

---

[101] Caen is a commune in north-west France. It is the capital of the Basse-Normandy Region.
[102] A small coastal village in south east Scotland, in Dumfries and Galloway.

be partially abandoned by the Americans, who went on to use the harbour for only small vessel unloading. Mulberry B remained operational for 10 months.

* * *

Leaving London after an extended period, the Evagoras travelled back up the east coast. She arrived in Middlesburgh on July 8th 1944 and I was signed off.

Edited by Katherine Hodgson

12 – The Eighth Voyage: The Beginning of the End

<u>The Empire Belle</u>: was a British Admiralty tug allocated to tow the Phoenix and Whale units of the Mulberry harbours in June 1944. Building began in 1943 by J Crown and Sons, Ltd in Sunderland. The Empire Belle was completed in February 1944 and commissioned by the Ministry of War Transport. After a long career which involved being permanently assigned to the British Admiralty in 1945 and sailing to locations including Singapore and Mumbai, the Empire Belle was sold to the Italian Navy in 1971 and scrapped in 1990.

The Memoirs of Alfred Hodgson

I signed on in Sunderland on 29th July 1944. When I arrived I was told I would be joining a tug for 'naval duties.' I had never even seen a tug before, let alone been on one. It was a coastal tug called Empire Belle and had been built for the Ministry of War Transport only a few months before I joined it. The other types of tug were harbour, river and deep sea. Upon arrival, we were told that the crew would help to repair the British Mulberry Harbour. Remnants of Mulberry A were being used to repair the sturdier Mulberry B at Arromanches. Mulberry B, which more than outlived its estimated 90 day life-span, was in use as a harbour for 10 months. It required continuous maintenance and following the storm on 19th June it too required considerable repair work. The breakwater devices used on the Mulberry Harbours were giant concrete caissons codenamed 'Phoenix.' These were built across the UK from 1943-44 and kept in storage until they were required. Once the caissons were in position, they were sunk. New caissons were being manufactured and towed to Normandy up until November 1944.

I had become used to the orderly life on past voyages: the communications; following the trail of command from the Admiralty, Convoy Commodore, Captain, Senior Radio Officer… and all on a fixed routine. Then, it just disappeared. I was the only Radio Officer and I had everything to do. Now, a series of job functions with a bewildering range of duties faced me. Most of my time would be spent on visual signalling by flag, Loud Hailer and Aldis Lamp. Instead of a Commodore in overall command we found that each function had a different supervisor, who changed frequently. We did not stay long in Sunderland and headed south where we would spend most of our time. The routine was quite hectic. We would collect an enormous piece of concrete, pull it up the English Channel and then across to the Arromanches beach where teams of workers would manhandle it into place. The perimeter of the area chosen as a harbour was defined by twenty or thirty sunken Merchant ships. These served as a breakwater. Although the whole thing seemed primitive it worked well and we had the satisfaction of seeing the tanks and lorries rolling along the harbour onto the beach. Bad weather was giving us more trouble than the enemy and it was very difficult to control these big lumps of concrete. Although our vessel was brand new it was not really able to deal with something which was designed *not* to float. The enemy action we did have to contend with was mostly Flying Bombs, but these were predominantly being aimed at land based targets. The anti-aircraft crews had by now developed a successful scheme of firing a barrage of shells in the path of the oncoming bombs. Unsurprisingly, this proved very effective if they managed to fire at the right place and in time. If the bombs were hit they would explode over the sea, where they could do no harm. I remember clearly seeing one of these bombs exploding in the sky, just ahead of us. We were pulling a gigantic lump of concrete towards Arromanches beach. What looked like a powerful shower of water in the sky was in fact a shower of shrapnel. It served as a chilling reminder that our bridge was open in every respect, and we did not have as much as a steel helmet for protection. The pundits at Whitehall had worked out that we would require a lifebelt, a whistle and a torch if we fell in the water. They also concluded that we could wrap ourselves up in a Duffle coat when it got cold but somehow they never got round to realising that we needed something more resistant if we were to protect ourselves from bombs.

Then followed a variety of tasks: towing barges; boats; ships; pipes; anything that had to be moved. We also found ourselves running a transport service, picking up parties of naval engineers and moving them from pillar to post. This particular voyage allowed me to become quite skilled with visual signalling on the Aldis Lamp. Nobody had ever taught me how to use the Lamp, it was something radio officers were expected to just pick up as they went along. The Navy, on the other hand, had been taught and specialised in this. Naval officers could send and receive messages at much faster speeds than any of us Merchant men. Most of the Royal Navy personnel were acutely aware of this and slowed down their messages to us, but all too often I found myself sending a signal back which asked them to repeat the message and do so 'slower, please.' The Army had, by this point, gone past the initial landing stage and had consolidated the beachheads. Although there had been a delay in taking Caen they were now on their way through Belgium and wanted to take up headquarters in Antwerp. However, before this could occur we had to open up the River Scheldt.[103] The Army dealt with the coastline of Belgium and the islands on the river and our role was to clear a channel of mines for the supply ships. Firstly, a fleet of wooden minesweepers were sent in, followed by the Merchant tugs slotting in behind. The tug was fitted out with paravanes which were two wires attached to each side of our bow with floats at the each end.[104] Sailing up the Schedlt, the paravane would divert any mines to the sides, where they would be caught in the snares of the wire and detonated by machine gun or rifle. We all moved backwards and forwards on the river until it was announced that it was clear. Although a fairly ingenious contraption, there was an acute awareness among the crew that we were not entirely sure if we did have the answer to the magnetic mine. Something could go wrong – mistakes could be made, mines could go off, undetonated. This was a pretty fiendish device whereby the magnetic pull of the ship's hull would trigger the detonator on the mine but with chilling German efficiency it would not detonate and would only click over one notch. There was no way of telling how many notches it had to click before

---

[103] The River Scheldt is a 270 mile long (435 km) river, starting in Northern France and outpouring in Holland. It flows across Belgium and passes through some strategically favourable European locations such as the Belgian textile centres, Flanders Plain and the French coalfields.

[104] An underwater towed 'glider' developed during WWI. They were originally constructed as an anti-mine weapon but later advancements formed explosive paravanes effective against submarines. They would usually be towed from the front of a ship.

detonation. Later we found that the answer was to use a 'degaussing' procedure where we would wind a thick electric cable around the hull of the ship to neutralise the magnetic force.

The Empire Belle soon helped to clear a passage into Antwerp. We tied up in a dockland where there was an eerie silence. An officer in the Belgian Resistance Army boarded, under the orders to safeguard us from any local hostility. He also acted as an interpreter. [105] We got to know him well and became very friendly. The other army personnel we met were Canadian. The first ships into Antwerp included an oil tanker (which stocked us all up) followed by a constant flow of support vessels with food, ammunition and medical supplies. Most of the communication was by loudhailer and our role at this point was to bring these ships alongside for unloading and then take them out again for the return journey. Apart from signalling and regular radio reception my own duties covered the maintenance and constant testing of the batteries and equipment – all to be recorded in a log for future inspection. The loudhailer batteries needed special attention as this equipment

---

[105] The Belgian Resistance – a blanket term used to describe clandestine movements working against the occupying government – had a military foothold in the Ardennes, with resistance fighters also based in urban areas gathering intelligence. Group G of the movement was responsible for sabotaging railways lines across Belgium and is often cited as the most successful of the movement's resistance cells. With approximately 3000 members, the group put out the electric lines across Belgium, costing the Germans 10 million man hours as a result.

was in constant use. The main transmitter batteries and lifeboat batteries had to be regularly discharged and then charged up again as they were rarely used. The Battle of the Bulge[106] was approaching and the Germans were doing their best to destroy the port of Antwerp with a hail of flying bombs. This was the era of the 'buzz bombs' so we got some warning of their arrival but the launching pads were fairly close by. [107] We were given permission to go ashore in Antwerp and move freely. There was little to attract a tired seamen ashore. Bars existed but the beer was terrible, coffee houses dotted the streets but the coffee was vile. There were shops but not much to entice even the most compulsive of shoppers. I wandered around the town and gazed in wonder at the silver altar of the cathedral which proudly flew the Belgian flag all day and night. There was a cinema and I went to a show which was a novelty. A couple of days later the cinema was struck by a bomb with a heavy death toll. There were not too many duties to do at night apart from bridge watch (to prevent sabotage) and it was on one of these watches that I truly believed my end had come. With the buzz bomb you could tell by the noise the direction of its flight. If you heard it overhead then you knew you were safe as it was going to fly over

---

[106] On 16 December 1944 the Germans launched a counter-offensive attack on the allied armies based in the quiet, poorly armed Ardennes region.

[107] This is a reference to the German flying bombs – the V1 bombs which made a buzzing noise as they approached. The buzz came from the bomb's pulse jet engine. The V-1 resembled a small aircraft. V-2 silent rockets began service in September 1944.

your head. However, on one occasion the noise cut out shortly before it reached me. This is it, I thought. It's going to hit me. I remember throwing myself on to the deck with a hastily conceived prayer. The bomb struck so very close that I really do not know how I escaped. Perhaps that prayer, however hastily conceived, worked a miracle after all. I took home a large piece of the bomb's casing as a souvenir and a reminder of how lucky I was to be alive.

A bad spell of weather hampered the air support which our troops needed. At one point the Germans launched an unexpected counter attack through the forests. The situation was severe and we were given orders to top up with fuel oil and stand by to receive five 'VIP persons' who were to be taken to London immediately. We were all on edge and I remember waking up in the morning to find the area deathly quiet. Gazing at Antwerp from the deck I was faced with a thick, black fog which hung over the city. It was not natural fog, it was a dense smokescreen. We were on tenterhooks and were standing by for a very hasty departure but the five VIP persons did not turn up and as time went by the smokescreen began to disperse, and with it our anxiety. The day went by and we heard that the crisis, although very close, had passed. On 13th August 1944 we had been sent to Southend where we discovered we were to be based at Gravesend. This pleased many of the crew who lived in that area. Handling a tug was a specialised job and it was convenient to keep the majority of the crew together. From Gravesend the Empire Belle travelled up to the Tyne, further north up the east coast of

Scotland and then through the Pentland Firth for a spell by Tobermory Bay. Most of our time was spent in the more traditional role of towing ships into harbour. Soon, we found ourselves back in the south coast hovering around the Belgian/ French coastline.

In January a tragedy intruded on our routine. While at Gravesend we had met, by chance, another tug called the Empire Rupert, a sister tug to Belle. It was similar to ours and the skipper and crew knew each other of old. It was a joyous reunion of friends and families and although I did not know any of them I was made very welcome. We heard many stories of past joint ventures and I leaned that the other skipper had acquired the habit of virtually living on his bridge when at sea, seating himself on a wicker armchair to do so. This was quite a story among tug circles and had become part of the folklore of their community. I remember being particularly struck by how young their cabin boy was, he could not have been more than in his early teens and had no doubt faked his age to join the crew but he was so proud to be with the older men. The reunion was short lived but nonetheless enjoyable for all. Quickly, we both headed for the French coast where there was always work to be done. The weather was not good. There was heavy fog and poor visibility. The 24th January 1945 started off like any other morning on the Empire Belle. As usual I put the radio receiver to the distress frequency and turned the volume right up. That's when I heard a distress signal shriek so loudly that it could only have come from close by. My heart sank when I heard it was from the Empire Rupert. We turned about

The Memoirs of Alfred Hodgson

immediately and headed for the given location with every ounce of steam we could muster. This was the only time I ever disobeyed a command from the Captain. He told me to call up the Empire Rupert and tell them we were coming but I stuck to the rigid rule that no radio signals were to be sent other than your own distress call for help. We were so close that it didn't take long for us to reach the wreckage. The decimated tug was clear to see, but no bodies lay in sight. As we circled the area I caught a glimpse of the remains of a wicker armchair. Seeing that chair produced a thick lump in my throat. We were soon joined by a naval vessel looking for survivors. The crew of the vessel were surprised to find us on site so soon. I sent him a message to say that we had not been sent to the scene but had answered the distress call. We had no further role in this tragedy and quickly went back to our duties, but the crew had been left almost paralysed by this loss. Men drifted through the ship like zombies, our ship growing heavy with the solemn atmosphere of a wake for a long time after. The official record for the Empire Rupert was terse and merely said 'sunk after collision 51.03 N, 01.32 E.'

It was getting close to the end of this voyage, which was to last about six months. Not long after the tragedy, we returned to sailing up and down the Thames to Gravesend and London. It was on this run that a very tolerant First Officer allowed me to take over the wheel as we roared full speed up the Thames. This was an exhilarating and thrilling experience. Despite being 23 years old and having the First

Officer hovering over me, the idea of taking the wheel gave me a tremendous sense of freedom and independence, as well as a real adrenaline rush.

The final leg of this voyage involved travelling back to Southampton and Portsmouth where we completed a variety of tasks for the Navy. Then, on 6th February 1945 we were signed off and I returned to Edinburgh feeling exhausted and drained: I had seen, done and experienced every possible sight, activity and emotion that this destructive war could give me. I had well and truly had enough. I felt as if I had nothing more to give.

13 – The Ninth Voyage: The End

<u>SS Norman Star</u>: Officially named the Norman Star 1, the vessel was built by Dunlop, Brenmer and Co. Ltd at Port Glasgow and was launched in 1919. It was launched as the SS Almeda. With a gross tonnage of 6817, the vessel was one of 38 pre-war ships in the famous Blue Star Line and one of only twelve to survive WW2. It was broken up in 1950 at Blyth.

The Blue Star Line was formed off the back of the Vestey family's successful butchery business. The Liverpudlian family were one of the first to introduce refrigeration into their shops. From there, they established a business which imported meat from South America. Refrigerated ships were required for this. The Blue Star Line was developed in 1919 specifically for the movement of eggs from China to Britain. The ships within the line did not originally contain the word 'star' in their name – this was added in 1920 with the first being the Albion Star. The line soon became renowned with the rich and famous for cruises in the Mediterranean. At the outbreak of war, the British government took control of the Blue Star Line vessels and used them as Merchant ships. Their refrigeration was ideal for transporting food.

This is the voyage I liked best of all. I was sent down to Southampton to join the Norman Star on 28th February 1945. By this time the Allied forces had virtually cleared the Germans out of France, Luxembourg, Holland and Belgium and were now penetrating Germany itself. The immediate threat had passed and the atmosphere was that of almost incredible relief. We would not be sailing in a convoy, partly because we would be faster than the submarines and partly because a convoy would slow us down too much. This was the standard procedure but was always a gamble – evident in the loss of 650 crewmen in the Blue Star Line vessels alone.

I was very impressed with the standard of the ship. The officers could all be identified by their uniforms while the stewards in the mess all wore an appropriate uniform. This was a far cry from the casual standards of the tramp steamers to which I had become accustomed. There were just over 60 men in our crew including a Master, four navigating officers, a cadet and three radio officers. The old traditional job titles from sailing ships days of bosun,[108] carpenter, lamptrimmer[109] and donkeyman[110] were still used for these relatively senior posts. There were more engineering officers than would have been expected

---

[108] The Bosun supervised the work of the able seamen who steered the ship, kept lookouts at sea and maintained the ship at sea and in port.

[109] As the name suggests, this seamen would maintain the ship's lamps ensuring there was enough oil in the lamps.

[110] Looked after all of a ship's auxiliary engines, rather than the vessel's main engine.

but this is due to the refrigeration equipment which had to be maintained.

3rd March 1945: we left Southampton. The Channel was still bustling with sea traffic but the big gun of St. Margaret's Bay and its German counterpart on the French Coast were silent. [111] There was no aircraft, no bombs, no U-Boats and no E-Boats.[112] We picked our way along the swept Channel gingerly because the mines were scattered like grass seed. These mines had been sown by the Allies, the French and the Germans, and it was going to be a long time before the minesweepers could be sent away. Soon we were on our own and setting a course south which would take us within sight of Ascension Island, then past the Cape Verde Islands and onwards to the Brazilian coast. Once in the South Atlantic a beautiful spell of soft and warm weather greeted us. There were no naval vessels watching; only an escort of dolphins who played games around the ship – leaping between the waves, rising up into the blue sky and cascading down again into the clear, aquatic floor beneath them. Further off into the distance we could see the water plumes of the sperm whales that frolicked and danced in the sea ahead. There was no aircraft overhead, just a lone albatross who stayed with us all the way. It was a peaceful period with just nature as our companion. Nevertheless we remained on a strict bridge watch

---

[111] The beach of St Margaret's Bay in Kent was heavily defended by anti-aircraft guns and heavy artillery.

[112] Schnelboot, which translates as 'fast boat', was a German torpedo ship which the allies nicknamed E-Boats. The 'E' stood for 'enemy'.

timetable, constantly on the look-out for the tell tale spume of a submarine periscope. However, the only disturbance we ever saw on the surface of the water was the incessant display from the flying fish. The sunsets, too, were impressive. The sun would slowly slink below the horizon, like an ember fizzling out. The daylight was then replaced by myriads of stars and shooting stars, they were best viewed when there was no moon but when the moon did rise we were given a different lighting display to excite the imagination. On morning watch we were treated to the magic of dawn as a glowing orb ascended from the horizon and transformed the whole scene once again.

Three weeks after we had left Southampton we reached the coastline of Brazil. By 30th March we arrived in Montevideo and travelled to the ship repair yards for extensive engine repairs. Sailing at maximum speed as often as possible was putting a heavy strain on the mechanical parts of the ship and although the engineers could execute emergency repairs, there was no substitute for a proper engine overhaul. We were given an overwhelmingly warm welcome from the British community who ran a Seaman's Mission in Montevideo. This provided us with a home from home. We stayed in Montevideo until 21st May and were there when VE Day was announced. On 8th May 1945 the announcement of a German surrender and allied victory in Europe created an authentic carnival atmosphere. It prompted the more enterprising members of the crew to set up a concert party. Loud blaring music, plenty of alcohol, laughter and a powerful and infectious wave of relief swept the Seamen's Mission and the Norman Star, as preparations for the concert party were being made. The local British community and the authorities were only too glad to help with the preparations. The crew had quite a bit of talent, both as singers and as comedians, while the British community were talented costume designers. The concert was held in the Victoria Hall and attended by HM Ambassador and his wife, and HM Consul and his wife. The local press even gave it a good review. I was unable to contribute – due to a spell of ill health, later diagnosed as a duodenal ulcer. Although every effort is made to provide a British Seaman medical help overseas, there is always a reluctance to sign seamen off sick and leave them in some foreign port. The seaman is put in the care of the local British Consulate who has the task of arranging a subsequent journey home to the UK under the classification of 'DBS' which stands for Distressed British Seaman. There is an inevitable and unjustified stigma attached to this designation, probably due to the fact that if a seaman 'jumped ship' overseas and was apprehended by the authorities, he would be deported back to his home country by the local consul as a DBS. Much later I found out that one of the Able Bodied Seaman also had a stomach ulcer at this time and was taken ashore to the British Hospital. He insisted on leaving to rejoin his ship and on doing so was made to sign a declaration stating: 'I hereby certify that I leave the hospital knowing that I have the risk of an ulcer haemorrhage or perforation and against the wishes of the doctor. By signing below... agrees that he returns on board entirely at his own risk with no liability for any consequences against the Master, Ship or Owners.'

I also retrospectively learned that a DBS was brought on board in Montevideo by the British Vice Consul, together with a Conveyance Order for his movement back to Britain. He was subsequently handed over to the Superintendent at Victoria Docks when we returned and a receipt was issued for him.

We arrived in Buenos Aires on 22nd May, the day after leaving Montevideo. It was here that I formed a friendship with an English family from Southampton. Mr and Mrs Middleton had sent their children to South America to escape the war. In the initial post-war years it was easy for me to keep in touch with them. In Buenos Aires the Norman Star underwent further repairs before heading south again to Patagonia on 4th July. It took us three weeks, until 28th July, to reach the approaches of the Magellan Straits.[113] We picked up a pilot at the entrance to the Straits to lead us through the first hazard – a narrow channel dotted with mud banks. We edged our way towards the second channel called the Segunda Angostura and anchored in the 'waiting area' at the entrance. There was only one ship per year that ventured along this route. We had an order to reach a remote freezer factory in Puerto Bories and collect the annual meat stock for the area. By now we had a chance to look around us and found that the initial scenery was bleak:

---

[113] Named after the Portuguese explorer, Ferdinand Magellan, who was the first person to circumnavigate the globe. The Strait belongs to Chile.

flat; dark; and desolate with Argentina to the north and Tierra del Fuego to the south. As we went further into the Strait the mountains of Patagonia came into view. As it was autumn south of the equator, the mountains peaks were merely snow-capped and looked quite majestic. This stretch of water was more winding than the first and as we travelled along it we found ourselves in a waterway, not much broader than a canal. This part of the journey was filled with twists and turns and when the ship eventually anchored for the night the war (and the rest of the world) seemed so very far away. The black night's sky and dark water melted into one and the hillsides in the distance – relatively barren of vegetation – stood by silently, making for a quiet evening. The local wildlife was harmless. There were wild geese, ducks and cormorants on land, while in the water lived white coated seals. Some of the crew decided to feed the ducks, attaching small nuggets of bread onto bent safety pins. They tied the pins onto string, before throwing the pin over the side.

After our first evening anchored in the Strait we rose early, at dawn, and continued on our journey. We eventually reached the channel which had the reputation as the most dangerous in the world. Named the Kirk Narrows, we had only about half a ships breadth to spare on either side with an island on one side and submerged rocks from the mainland on the other. The channel at either end is comparatively wide, meaning that a very powerful current complete with whirlpools rushes through this opening at ten knots. This made it impossible for the Norman Star to get through. However, the water was tidal and the locals had a system for us to follow. A tug arrived at an appointed time and we approached the entrance. The tug would get as close as it could to the Narrows and then we both stopped to wait for the tide to turn. This opened a narrow window of only ten minutes when we could move before the force of water would build up again. We built up a full head of steam and the tug blew on its whistle when the tide began to turn, then we moved up and hugged the edge of the Narrows until we heard a second whistle to tell us that the tide was as slack as it was going to be. After that we raced through at full speed. Time passes very quickly in these circumstances and thankfully the ship got through within the ten minute period. Unfortunately passing through the Kirk Narrows was not the only difficult and complex manoeuvre to be executed. On breaking through we were faced with an island right in front of us. A 'Double S' bend had to be made to stay clear of the island. The need for a pilot aboard was never greater as we continued to twist and turn, avoiding the mud on either side of the waterway. It was at this time that we saw an enormous glacier. The huge river of ice, all the way down the mountainside, glinted blue in the sunshine. It stood in sharp contrast to the surrounding cliffs and acted as an ominous warning of the natural dangerous in the channel. No longer was the prime concern submarines, but rather powerful currents and extreme landscapes.

The freezer plant was situated in the middle of a small village, with the port of Puerto Natales about two miles away. The plant was used as the collection

The Memoirs of Alfred Hodgson

point for the cattle from all the ranches in the area. The meat was then sent to Port Natales for distribution. Since the Norman Star was a refrigerated cargo liner we were able to go directly to the freezer plant to stock up. As it was a meat packing station with a village built round it, our arrival caused quite a stir. A crowd gathered round the wooden quay to watch us anchor and come ashore. When the crew did walk the streets any number of doors and windows were opened to allow the locals to view the strangers. The village itself reminded me of a Wild West story with mud roads, tin or wooden houses and paraffin lamps dotted about. There were dogs everywhere, all shapes and sizes but mostly Great Danes or Alsatians. If it was a mild day then we would slosh around in inches of mud and if it was cold then a thick layer of ice coated the entire village. In spite of all the snow and ice, it was easy to overcome the cold by simply slipping on an extra layer, a scarf, and a pair of gloves. I remember on one occasion walking along the shore of the bay and feeling quite hot, but I noticed that the surface of the water on the shoreline had frozen over. The temperatures were erratic and varied. The local town of Puerto Natales was only a few miles away and we visited it also. Only two buildings in the town were solid structures: the brick hospital and the stone church. The church, not surprisingly, was a Catholic one and was unexpectedly large for such a small, remote community. There was even a local choir comprised of young boys. And the church's central heating consisted of two strategically placed stoves, a simple answer to keeping the congregation warm.

Meat packing duties continued throughout the weekend. I was off duty on the Sunday morning and decided to attend Mass. This meant I walked. Although the countryside was wild and rather forbidding there was no risk of me losing the way because there was a narrow gauge railway from the packing station to the port and I simply walked along it. This was a fairly difficult trek because the space between the sleepers on the rail line did not match my normal footsteps, and for obvious reasons I had to watch where I was putting my feet. On this occasion I was taken by surprise by the chivalry of my shipmates. I knew that going to Mass meant I would be late for lunch on board. Our meals were at a fixed time and started when the Master sat down. When I returned from church I went straight to my cabin, but I had only just stepped through the door when a steward knocked and greeted me with an invitation from the Master to join him for lunch. I felt quite humbled and soon found that instructions had been given to keep my lunch hot and serve me when I returned from church. This was simply unheard of. Discipline required a rigid acceptance of meal times. Perhaps this exception reflected the surprise at, and even possibly the appreciation of, my voluntary journey to church. Such an act did not just require the approval of the Master but also the active cooperation of the Chief Steward and his staff.

There was a train at the meat packing plant that was exactly like those comic trains often in Punch magazine.[114] It was so very small with little wheels yet a huge, high stack bulged out of the cabin. When it moved off it made more noise and let off more steam than the Flying Scotsman but it effectively provided a freight service from packing station to the port. The chief means of transport for the locals was on horseback and gauchos were regularly seen on foot or horseback. A friend and I were invited into one of the tin plate houses and I was surprised to find how comfortable it was inside. The walls had plasterboard covering to keep out draughts, the ceilings were made of wood and linoleum covered the floors. The house was kept warm by a large range which burned logs all day and night, all year round. Everything was spotlessly clean and water was gathered from the roof in a barrel. The fundamental lighting source was from a paraffin lamp although the family also had a storage battery to provide light if required, and to power the wireless. They could charge this battery from a small generator worked by a miniature windmill. According to the maritime charts, the whole country was dotted with radio masts which, presumably, was the basic communication system. The family in the house were of Italian descent but we never learned any more about their family history because the language barrier limited our conversation. Doggerel Spanish was spoken on our side and basic English on theirs. Our

---

[114] A British satirical magazine renowned for its political cartoons. Punch cartoonist David Low was a prominent anti-appeaser and many of his anti-Nazi cartoons were highly controversial in the 1930s. The weekly magazine was formed in 1841 and closed down in 1992.

hosts cooked us a meal which consisted of home cured bacon (tasty but tough), some delicious but mysterious soup, fried eggs, chips and steak which again took a lot of chewing. The meal was rounded off with tinned fruit and coffee and throughout there was a constant flow of sweet red wine. I cannot remember how we repaid our hospitality but it was probably with cigarettes which had become my universal currency.

At that time of year the countryside would usually be windswept, but we were fortunate to get very little wind at all. The water in the bay was as smooth as glass and with the whole area surrounded by snow-capped mountains we were treated to a picture postcard scene. After a few weeks based in Puerto Bories we left and retraced our route out through the winding waterways, always very conscious of the numerous wrecks which were scattered along the way. When we were passing through the Segunda Angostura Channel we intercepted a distress message from another British ship at the end of the channel where it broadens out. The ship had run aground on one of the mud-banks and we offered to stand by to provide any assistance required. However, we proceeded on our voyage when we were given an assurance that a tug from Punta Arenas was attending instead.[115] By the end of July we found ourselves back at the entrance of the Straits and from there we headed north. We were not to leave this part of the world without another few remarkable sights. One morning there was an unusual sunrise. The sky was fiery red

---

[115] The capital city of Chile's most southern region, Magallanes and Antartica Chilena.

which was reflected by bands of cloud, stretching half way round the horizon and interspersed with streaks of green and yellow. Everything witnessed that dawn had a deep red tint and although it only lasted a few minutes it was profoundly moving. The 2nd August 1945 is a date which sticks firmly in my mind, for it marks the beginning of another remarkable natural spectacle. We were only two days away from reaching Montevideo when the event occurred. The red sunrise returned and the general consensus on board was that this meant bad weather was to follow. However, the day passed without any violent atmospherics. The next day broke slightly misty and by mid-morning we were running into fog banks. By the evening we were caught in thick fog which lasted for days. There would have been no real problem had the fog just passed within a few days but on the last day of it there were severe atmospherics. That could only mean one thing: an electrical storm was developing. There was thunder, lightning and hailstones the size of peas all accompanied by gale force winds. The weather then developed into a series of squalls. There was one which came on very suddenly and transformed everything to a bright green colour – the sea, the sky. It was as if even the air itself turned green. I thought at the time that this must be an example of 'St. Elmo's Fire' and it was decidedly spooky.[116] The Norman

---

[116] St Erasmus of Fornia, otherwise known as St Elmo is the patron saint of sailors. An electrically charged conductor which is ionized by a fluid will give off an electrical discharge, known as a coronal discharge. During a storm this will cause glowing plasma to form from sharp, pointed objects e.g. a ship.

Star was run aground on a sandbank that evening – one squall had caused so much chaos and distracted us greatly. It is quite an uncanny sensation when you run aground. We were used to the undulating motion of the water and then, without warning, all motion stops. You feel rather helpless. Apparently the ship's compass had been affected by the electrical storm and although we tried to get off we were stuck. The wind worked against us also, blowing us further on to the sandbank. The wind changed its course just before dark and in a very short space of time. If it had only been stronger it would have helped us. This change of wind direction was a danger signal in itself and as the night drew to a close the wind grew stronger and stronger. We were, of course, in radio contact with the shore and at about half past eight in the evening we were given a hurricane warning. Everyone on board had been hoping for a wind to help us off the sandbank, but a hurricane was unwanted as it could easily overturn us. It's true what they say – be careful what you wish for. About an hour after receiving the warning the hurricane broke, complete with thunder, lightning and driving rain. The wind reached a terrifying 90 miles per hour but luck was with us this time and the storm had the desired effect of raising the water level to the point that we slid off the mud bank and into deeper water. We were off the sandbank and back on water but the weather was too bad to proceed.

By this time we were overdue in Montevideo and our bunkers were running low. The ship was unstable and it was not long before there was a breakdown in the engine room. However, fortune favoured us yet again and the engineers managed to fix the engines promptly. The weather abated and we sailed into Montevideo on 5th August without any further mishap. After a quiet night in Montevideo – enjoying a few, chilled beers in a quiet bar overlooking the Atlantic – we set off again. This time the Norman Star would be terminating in Britain and our route home involved travelling up the coast of South America. The weather held for a couple of days but we soon ran into a further succession of tropical squalls, slowing down our journey time. After about a week of battering through the storms, we arrived in Pernambuco in north east Brazil for bunkering. The ship was only anchored there for a few hours and it was agreed among the crew that there was not much in the town itself. It was old, rather scrappy and built on peninsulas joined by bridges. We left in a spell of fine weather with a very welcomed cool breeze and settled into a pleasant, routine peacetime voyage home. The Board of Trade had prescribed a format for the journey home. A contract was signed by the ship owners and each member of the crew upon setting out. It was a contract of employment for the voyage and complied with international law. Full details of the ship, the owners and the crew were written out together with the minimal requirement to be supplied by the shipping company. If there had to be any alteration to the contract due to death, illness or desertion etc. then that had to be recorded by the local British Consul at the first port of call. It was mandatory that the same agreement was produced at the end of the voyage and again signed by all parties.

14th August, 20.30 hours: our journey was interrupted by an official announcement over the wireless. Japan had fallen and the Second World War had ended. All the neighbouring ships broke radio silence to send out the 'V for Victory' signal and the relief was difficult to appreciate. The next morning the Captain asked all his officers to assemble on the Bridge Deck, outside his cabin, and drink a toast to peace. Sherry was passed around and we all exchanged approving glances. The Captain had broken one of the most basic of maritime rules – no alcohol at sea, but if a rule was to be broken this was the most marvellous time to do so. After spending six years battling a Fascist enemy, fighting against the depravity and evil in man it seemed rather fitting to have a light tipple.

'Here's to peace, thank God we are still alive.' The Captain announced sombrely, and then raising his glass in the air he released a quiet cheer.

The threat of any rogue U-Boats lurking the Atlantic had now passed and the blackout restrictions relaxed. We rang the ship's bells after a silence of six years and peacetime lookouts were posted. It was like living in a different world, a world of peace. A world where constant battle, fear, death and destruction did not permanently infect your mind: your vision; your hearing; your thoughts.

Until then we did not know which port we would be sailing into when we reached Britain. Once peace had been announced we were informed over the radio that it would be London. Earlier in the voyage, the crew held a sweep on where the terminating port would be. I drew Cardiff and had this been correct, I would have won the equivalent of £82 in today's terms.[117] But I had no regrets as we headed for Victoria Docks in London.

Our final lap took us over the Bay of Biscay where it was warm and calm, with only a distant memory of the U-Boat bays and enemy naval harbours which used to stalk that area. That fine weather – so glorious, reeking of victory and glory – took us all the way up to the Thames on what was by then a very familiar route after another very memorable voyage.

---

[117] As estimated in 2014.

Edited by Katherine Hodgson

14 – The Tenth Voyage: Clearing up

<u>Josiah A. Mitchell</u>: Built Avondale, New Orleans and delivered in March 1945. Gross tonnage 2905, she was sold to China in 1947 and subsequently scrapped. The ship was named after a 19th century American ship's captain.

US Maritime Commission: this executive commission was established by Congress in 1936 under the Merchant Marine Act of the same year. This replaced the United States Shipping Board which was formed during the Great War. The Commission was created to design and build 500 new Merchant ships over a 10 year period.

'This was my last voyage…'

3rd October 1945. I was in Poplar, London. I joined an American Coastal Cargo ship of the US Maritime Commission, called *Josiah A Mitchell*. The ship was newly built; shiny, high quality and modern, having been finished in March 1945. It had all the glossy fittings, fixtures and furnishings to be expected from the world's richest country. It was well stocked with the very highest standard of food, drink, confectionary and cigarettes. The voyage was to last six months and was to follow a fairly tedious routine. We were making several trips to the Scheldt. Leaving from Southampton to Le Havre, then onto Antwerp, and then to Bremerhaven. Each trip would involve taking supplies to the military who would be remaining in Germany for some time.

During the voyage I, like many others on board, had vivid flashbacks to earlier trips on this very route. Back to a time when what dominated the mind was warfare and survival. But now, the constant fear of death, and the lurking assault of violence had all gone. Now, there was an overwhelming desire to move onto the next equally repetitive task. The peace and quiet experienced on the new trip was a welcomed thing. There was little to attract us to either the French or Belgian towns that we visited, as all that remained in them were remnants of the war. A war we all craved to get away from greatly. My work on board was mostly visual signalling and clerical work. I recorded the movement of the seamen who were constantly changing, due to the fact that we were in port so often. During this period I wrote enquiring about when I could be discharged from the Merchant Navy. I learned there was going to be no difficulty in being discharged, and I was pleased to find this out.

We were frequent and regular visitors to Southampton and there I was able to renew my friendship with the Middleton family whom I had met in Buenos Aires, and who lived in Fareham. Spending time with the family gave me a warm and comforting glimpse back into civilian life.

I was signed off on 8th April 1946 in Southampton. I returned home to Edinburgh during my brief spell of leave and once that passed I reported to the Mercantile Marine Office in Leith on 29th April 1946. There I was given a 'Certificate of Discharge from Merchant Navy Service' on the grounds of 'Termination of War Service'. HM Customs and Excise gave me 107 clothing coupons to set myself out as a civilian and integrate back into British post-war society. [118] The Registrar of Shipping in Cardiff sent me the medal ribbons for the Africa Star with Clasp and the Atlantic Star with Clasp. I had already been given the '39-43 Ribbon which was subsequently known as '39-45 Star. The medals themselves did not reach me until very much later, but once they had it drew a final double line to this part of my life.

---

[118] Rationing in Britain continued into 1954, with clothes coupons finishing in 1949.

15 – Conclusion

"The war meant a big gap in my lifestyle, a break from the family traditions and comforts that I had spent my childhood and adolescence becoming accustomed to."

Some claim that writing about a painful event in your life can be therapeutic. My grandfather has found this to be true. Writing about The Second World War – a global phenomenon which not only brought him pain, but was intense, lengthy and life changing – has indeed been a pleasant task for him. In writing down his memories and openly discussing them with me, he has been forced to take stock of the events and emotions of that time. Even for a mere on-looker like me, it has been a greatly rewarding experience. I have been able to consolidate much of my knowledge about the war and have relished in all of the new information my grandfather and I have come across. Over the past two and a half years, we have spent many a long afternoon huddled over the computer together. We have talked, taken notes, typed frantically, dug out old documents and photos, and researched meticulously. It has been a long and sometimes frustrating process. But in completing these memoirs to a published standard we have given a gift to each other. And it is a completely unique gift which will remain accessible for years to come. The patience and openness my grandfather has shown me has made that gift possible, and I am truly grateful for that.

* * *

Once signed off for the final time Alfred returned to a different life. Long gone were the days of lazy strolls through Princes Street Gardens, nights spent huddled over the Magic Lantern with his siblings, and afternoons spent basking in the beauty of Edinburgh's Public Library. These habits and hobbies, which were the mark of his comfortable life in Edinburgh, had crumbled with the outbreak of war. Or more specifically, the end of the Phoney War. Returning to Edinburgh after his last voyage, Alfred was aware of the quiet emptiness which hung over the city streets. On the surface, however, not much had changed. Joppa still looked much the same – little physical damage had occurred. Life still moved at a similar pace. Clydebank, in the west of Scotland, had been most badly affected during the Blitz and it was in these industrial, working classes areas where the physical consequences of war where felt the most. [119] My grandfather quickly returned to work for Howden and Molleson. There he worked in the firm's auditing division, spending much of his time auditing coal mines for the Coal Board.

"Edinburgh was still considered the central authority in Scotland. That's why Edinburgh auditors

---

[119] The term 'Clydebank Blitz' refers to the nights of 13th and 14th March 1941, when the industrial area of Clydebank in Glasgow suffered devastating levels of bombing. On one of those evenings Alfred had been on fire watch in Edinburgh.

went to the west of Scotland. There were dozens of coal mines across the central west area."

Rarely based in the firm's head office in Edinburgh, he spent most of his time in the city centre of Glasgow. After a couple of years of tedious and tiresome commuting to and from Glasgow by car, Alfred caved in and rented a room in Glasgow.

"I made new friends, ran in a new circle of people and lived in a new environment."

Living full time in Glasgow meant a return to a steady way of life. It truly was a fresh start following the erratic nature of wartime naval life. Stability had been achieved for the first time since 1941. The new life he forged for himself in Glasgow meant the chance to create brand new hobbies and traditions.

It was whilst visiting a mutual friend's house in 1953 that my grandparents met. Alfred and Josephine were married two years later in St Peter's Church in Partick, Glasgow. The first of their four children was born the following year, in 1956 – a decade after the final voyage. As a Chartered Accountant, Alfred began working with General Motors in the 1960s. He enjoyed a long and successful career with the company, taking advantage of the job's numerous opportunities to travel widely. The idea of travelling – seeing and experiencing new places – was the central factor in influencing him to enrol in the navy. It seemed that his passion for travel remained throughout his adult life. Following his retirement from General Motors, Alfred ran his own small accountancy firm with two friends. He continued working into his late

80s. Today, he enjoys a peaceful life in the south of Glasgow. He devotes his time to his family. He enjoys the company of his four children and seven grandchildren, and the many other family members and friends present in his life.

Katherine Hodgson